JANET SCOTT

ARTIST

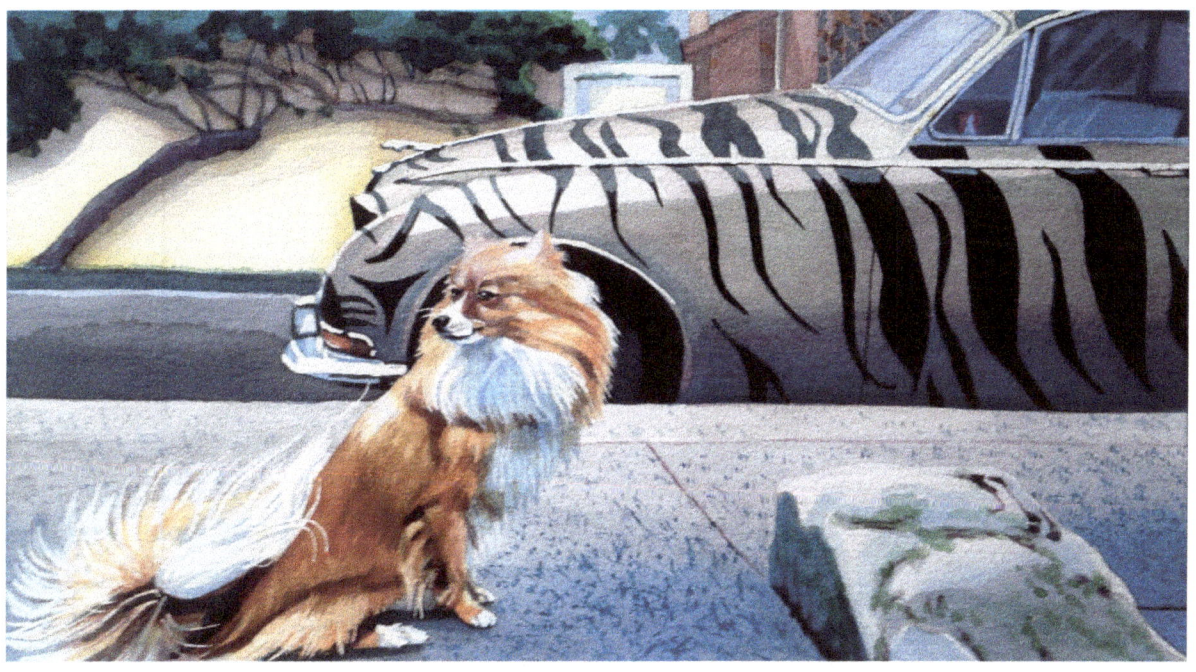

Artist : Janet Scott

JANET SCOTT
ARTIST

My personal recollections
compiled by

briann kearney

Editor
Sue Binney

First Edition 2022
ISBN 978 1 4716 9741 8

© Jessica Douglas, Miranda Douglas & Akea Scott

JANET SCOTT

The Australian born arist Janet Scott (10.8.1941 - 23.4.2018) (aka Janet Catherine Scott, Janet C. Scott and, when I first met her, by the diminutive name of Janey and her husband's name of Douglas) is the descendant of early Australian pioneers including those involved with Cobb & Co. and the pastoral industry in the Northern Territory. At one time, along with her brother, Janet visited her ancestors' former holding in the N.T. to apologise for any mistreatment that may have occurred in the past. The Indiginous people who were living there of course did not know, nor remember, Janet's relatives but as she said, with extreme politeness they accepted the apology offered by her and her brother and invited Janet to enjoy a never forgotten experience in the Outback.

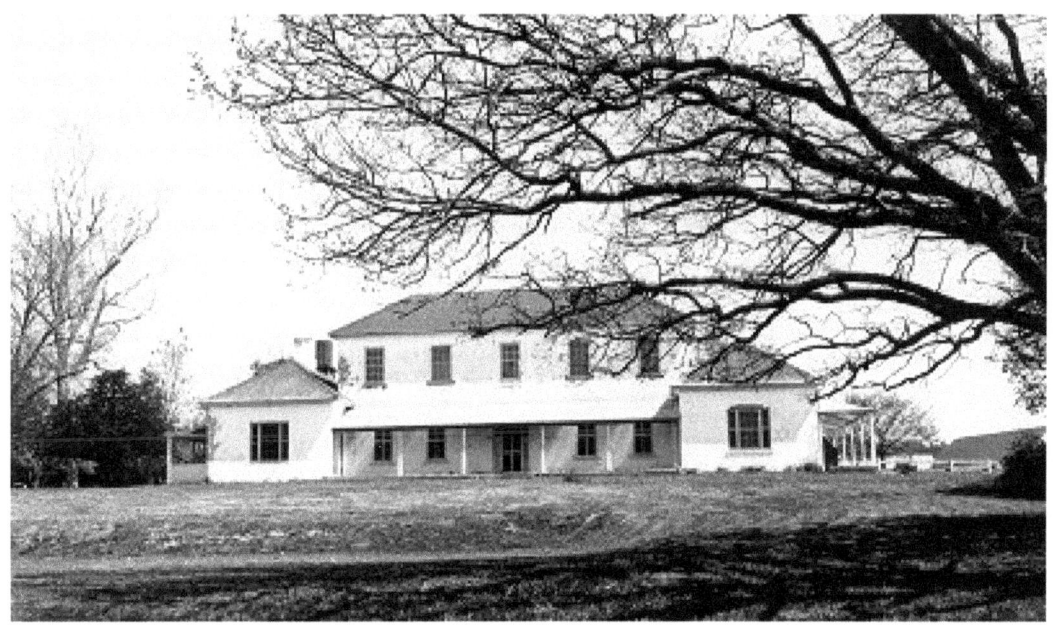

"Carwoola"

In many, many ways Janet was a country woman - she was born in country New South Wales and grew up on her family's property - "Carwoola".

Use of the name Carwoola dates from at least 1850 and may be a derivation of the word Carrowillah, mentioned as early as 1827.

Carwoola or Carrowillah is said to be an Aboriginal word for "the meeting of the waters on the plain", a lyrical, apt title because Carwoola station lies on river flats between hills bisected by the Molonglo River, which is fed by numerous streams. The meaning may also be found in the fact that Primrose Creek, a southern tributary of the Molonglo, meets that river to the north-east of St. Thomas' Anglican Church, built on Carwoola land.

The homestead complex with its wide variety of out-buildings in both stone and slab, was described in 1866 as "the magnificent property of Thomas Rutledge, Esq. Which may be termed the model farm Par Excellence of NSW. It could equally be described as the nineteenth century homestead par excellence because of its completeness."

Carwoola is an early colonial homestead complex set in an impressive rural landscape of natural and man-made elements. The site has important historical associations and was a centre of rural hospitality in the district during the later part of the 19th century. It has significant historic values as evidence of early pastoral development and achievement.

In 1929 the homestead was described as a "comfortable two storied stone building" ... The house has 16 rooms in the main building, including a magnificent billiard room. Outside the house one finds pretty gardens laid out in striking formation above which tower beautiful English trees including elm and oak .

An historian writing in 1938 claimed that The Molonglo River was known to the Aborigines as the Yealambidgee, meaning a chain of waterholes, and the plains on the watershed of this river above Carwoola Gap were known as as Molinggoolah, which name has been corrupted into the modern Molonglo. Moolinggoolah was subdivided by the Aborigines into Carwoola (still retained) and Enwoola (now Foxlow), meaning the centre and the end of the plain below and above the junction of the Tirralilly River.

The country property which today is 5,000 acres, was owned by the Scott family for maybe half a century - from the 1920s until 1972.

Although she grew up on the family property in Bungendore the family also had a holiday house at spectacular Palm Beach and Janet screened some of the Super 8 footage of her school holidays at this beautiful location.

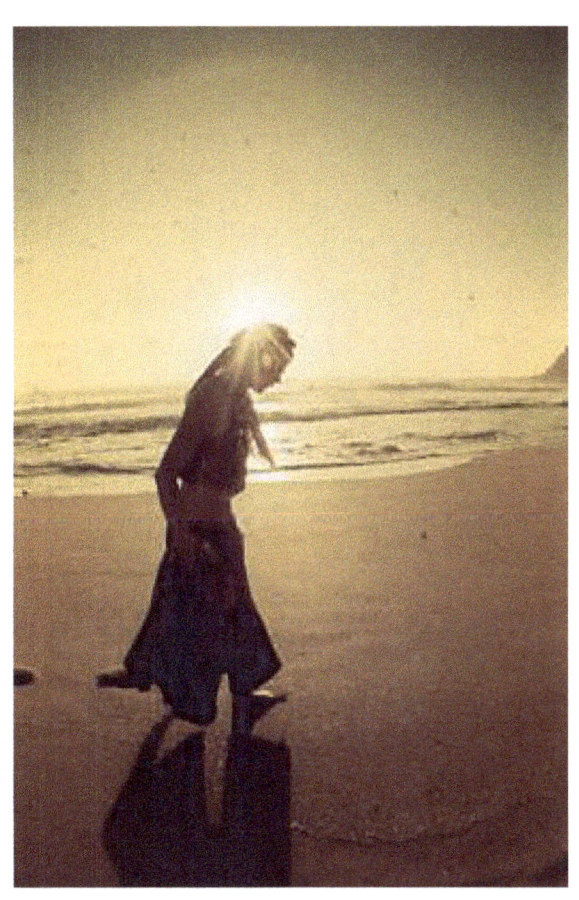

"Sunrise at Palm Beach" (1969)
Photograph : Robert C. Crock

Schooling was at Frensham School, Mittagong in the Southern Highlands of New South Wales. Founded by Winifred Mary West in 1913 and named after Ms West's birthplace - Frensham, Surry.

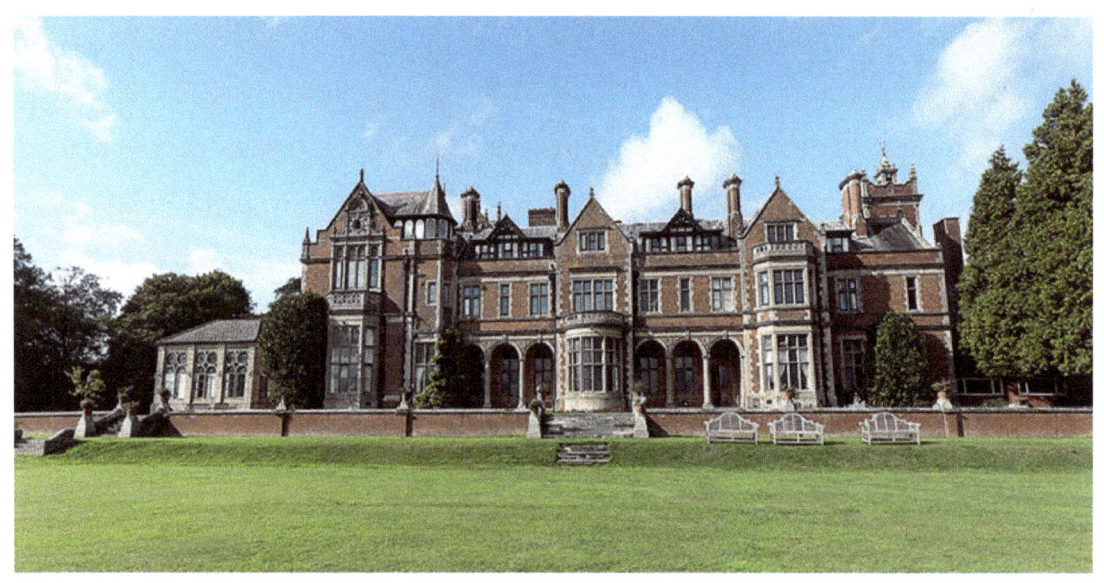

Date and photographer : Unknown

In 1934 the New Zealand born photographer Harold Pierce Cazneau published a book of photographs of the school and its students - THE FRENSHAM BOOK - which is now held by the National Library of Australia. Mr. Cazneau was elected a member of the London Salon in 1921 and was the first Australian (his mother was Australian) to become an Honorary Fellow of the Royal Photographic Society.

Harold Cazneau's photo of Frensham School students in the school in 1934.

Frensham School's Old Girls alumni includes : Marion Hall Best, Kate McClymont, Dr. Catherine Hamlin AC, Jane Matthews AO, Christine Davy MBE., Linda Buckingham and Janet Scott.

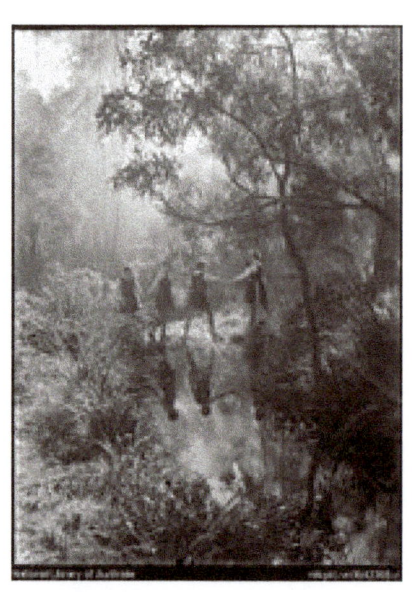

On finishing school Janey proceeded to study art from 1960 - 1963 at the East Sydney Technical College, Forbes St., Darlinghurst, Sydney now known as the National Art School. Although not necessarily during Janet's study period, Technical College students included Robert Klippel, John Coburn, Tony Tuckson, Margaret Olley, Charles Blackman and Bert Flugelman along with teachers such as John Passmore, Charles Blackman, William Dobell, Bim Hilder, Ralph Balson, and Bessie Guthrie.

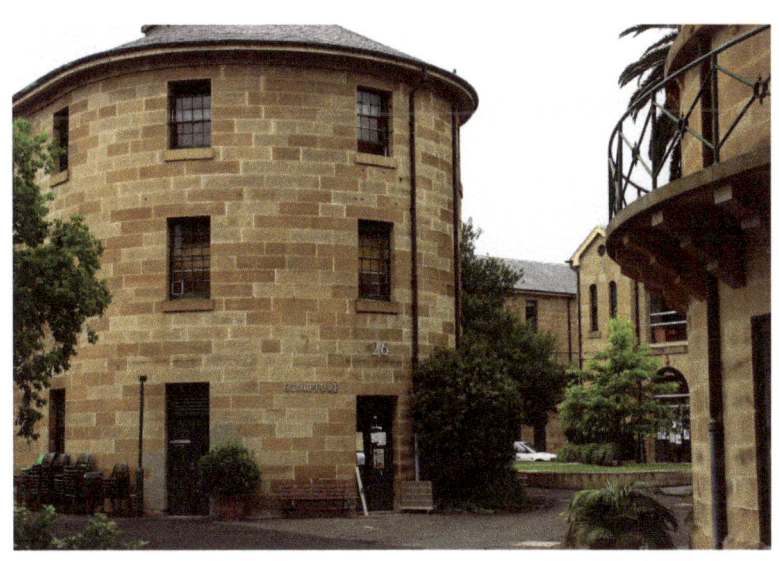

"Sculpture" Building
East Sydney Technical College, Darlinghrst
sydney-eye.blogspot.com

At the completion of her Arts degree in 1963 Janey returned to Canberra and undertook an Art & Design degree at the Australian National University, during which period she married and had two children, Jessica and Miranda Douglas. She married quite young but this was common in those days when becoming a "wife" was a career path…though not really for Mrs. Douglas.

Janey was awarded The 1965 Australian National University Art Prize resulting in her drawings being represented in the Australian National University collection.

The Drawing Prize showcases and celebrates the breadth and depth of drawing practice within the Australian National University - School of Art & Design.

In 1966 Janey was awarded another National University Art Prize when she entered as part of the Australian National University's Group Exhibition.

1967 - Janey Douglas held her first Solo Exhibition :
SILK SCREENED FABRICS
at the Cinema Centre Gallery,
Now part of the Canberra Museum & Gallery, Canberra, A.C.T.

By 2022 CMAG (as it is called) serves a unique role - it is a place to experience the diverse history and contemporary culture of the Canberra region and through this to gain a deeper understanding of Australia's dynamic culture in its global setting."

CMAG

From 1969 - 1971 and following her graduation from the Australian National University, Janey taught painting, drawing & printmaking at the Canberra Technical College, A.C.T.

A further 2 solo Canberra, A.C.T. exhibitions followed :

1970   Painting (Unnamed exhibition)
          Australian Sculpture Gallery, Canberra

1975   Drawings (Unamed exhibition)
          Australian National University - School of Art & Design -
          Griffith Gallery, Canberra

'The School of Art & Design Gallery critically frames contemporary art and design practice and presents graduate and post graduate work in a professional gallery context reflecting the international profile of the School.

The Gallery also hosts the end of year Graduation Exhibition which displays the achievements of graduating students achieving awards..."

Janey expanded her painting and drawing skills to include producing events and as the Founder and President of THE SALT WORKSHOP ASSOCIATION she aimed at bringing artists from all media and many cities together to join local Canberran artists to create multi-talent performances.

In 1972 Janey produced "SALT SPACE ADVENTURE" for children and "SALT DAY" for adults which included her fellow East Sydney Tech student Herbert "Bert" Flugelman (1923 - 2013) and the renowned Melbourne electronics musician Stevie Dunstan (1941 - 1984) to join musicians from Canberra.

Bert Flugelman was born in Vienna, Austria arriving in Australia in 1938 and from 1943 - 1946 Mr. Flugelman served in the Australian army (non-combative duties). He was an academic and prominent visual artist who is known for his stainless steel geometric sculptures.

Australian born Stevie Dunstan (aka Steve Dunstan, Stephen Dunstan) was a Melbourne based electronic composer, musician, synthesiser inventor and member of the Hoadley family responsible for staging the Hoadley Battle of the Bands competitions.

Stephen Jones PhD wrote in 1974 "Dunstan, a composer, jazz musician and mystic source of creative energy had been making and playing electronic instruments for ten years and his music and his instruments were a fascinating and unique reflection of Dunstan's nature." Stevie's "Saturn" synthesiser shows the level of his artistic talent. It is quite the most amazing piece of work for 1968 - 1969 or 2022.

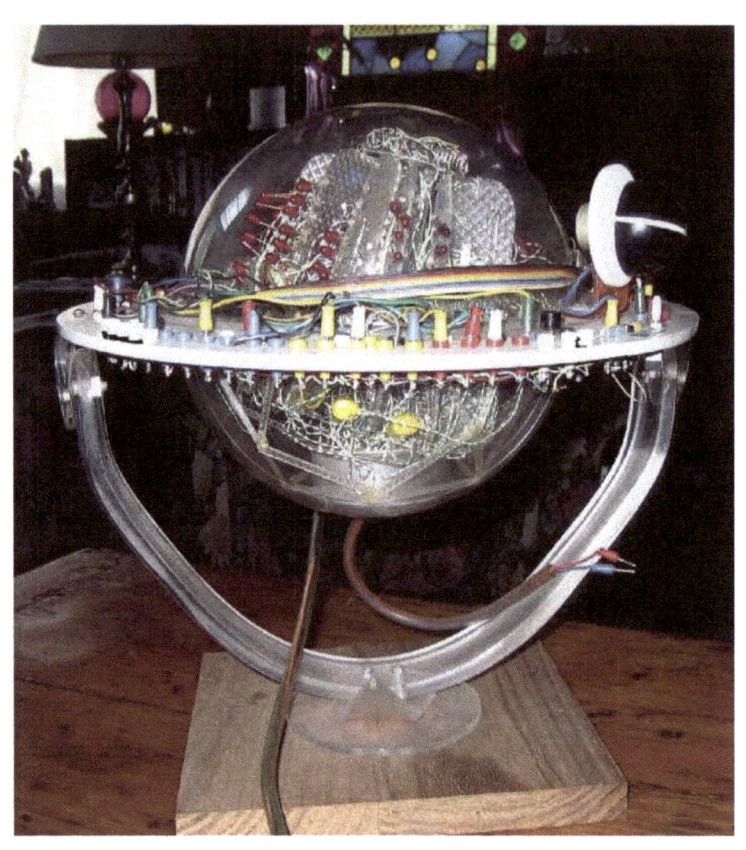

Steven Dunstan's "Saturn" synthesiser
Photograph : Stephen Jones
Plate 28 (figure 8.6)
Held in the collection of John Hansen

1973 saw Ms Douglas produce "EXPLORATIONS" with the Youth Theatre for Kids, Canberra (nka - Canberra Youth Theatre).

Janey was an early foundation member of the Canberra Youth Theatre which began as Canberra Children's Theatre then the Youth Theatre Workshop and in the 1970s was based in Reid House.

In September, 1973 President Douglas produced THE ALL SENSES BALL - THE FIRST DAY OF SPRING with the SALT WORKSHOP ASSOCIATION and the Canberra Youth Theatre at the Albert Hall, Canberra, sponsored by Australia Council for the Arts and televised by the Australian Broadcasting Commission. Quite an entrepreneurial coup.

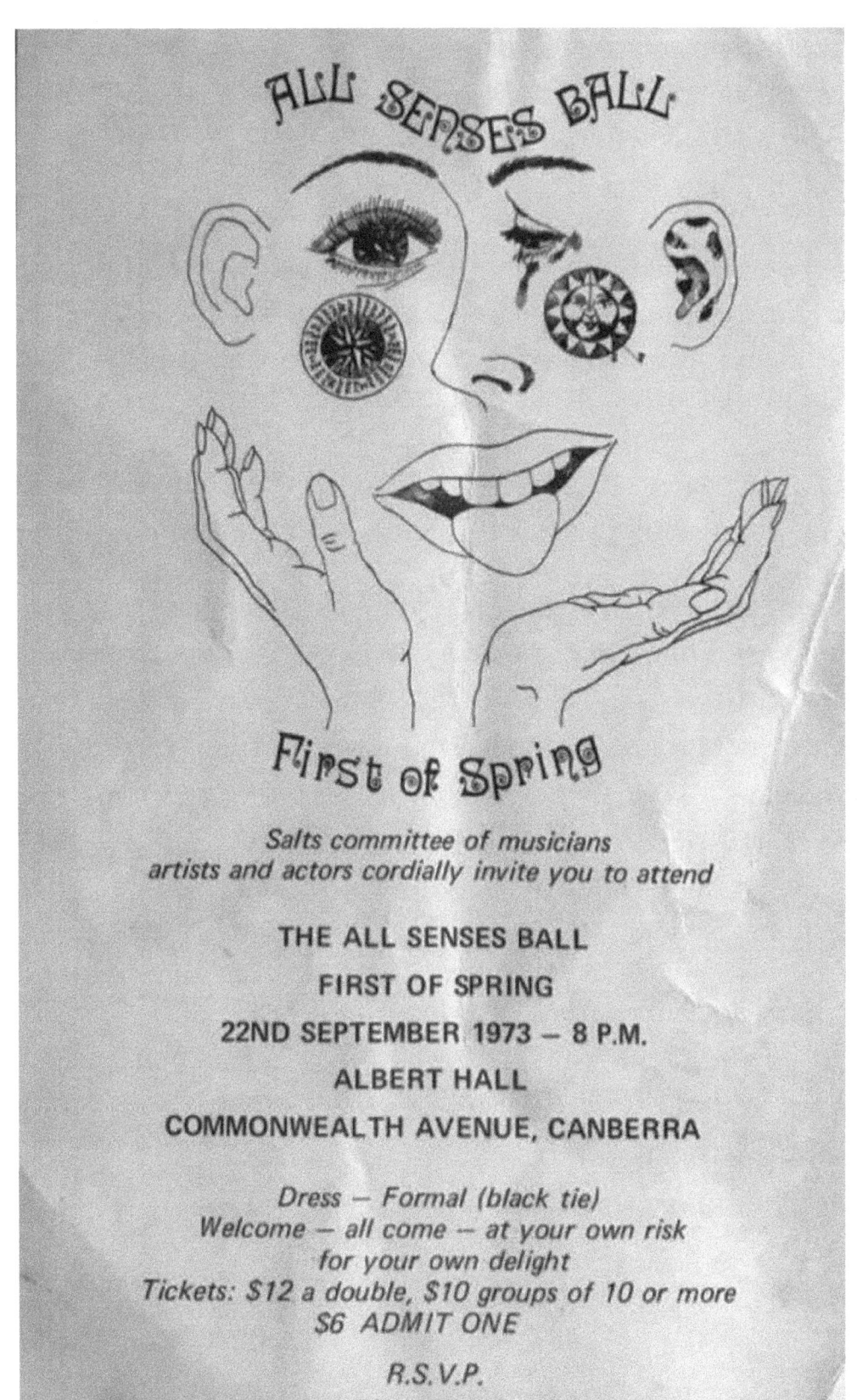

ALL SENSES BALL

First of Spring

*Salts committee of musicians
artists and actors cordially invite you to attend*

THE ALL SENSES BALL

FIRST OF SPRING

22ND SEPTEMBER 1973 — 8 P.M.

ALBERT HALL

COMMONWEALTH AVENUE, CANBERRA

*Dress — Formal (black tie)
Welcome — all come — at your own risk
for your own delight
Tickets: $12 a double, $10 groups of 10 or more
$6 ADMIT ONE*

R.S.V.P.

Ms. J. DOUGLAS, PRESIDENT
SALT ASSOCIATION, 18 BINDEL PLACE, ARANDA, A.C.T.

Poster Artist : Janey Douglas

This production combined artists from Sydney, Melbourne and Canberra and featured Mic Conway and the Captain Matchbox Whoopee Band plus Stevie Dunstan.

Mic Conway (Captain Matchbox) and the Captain Matchbox Whoopee Band was formed in Melbourne in 1969 as a jug band by Mic with his brother Jim Conway, Mick Fleming, Dave Huggard, David Isom, Jeffey Cheesman and John McDiamid. In 1971 they appeared in Tim Burstall's movie - STORK (1971)

In 1974 Janey produced "KROMOS - THE FIRST DAY OF SPRING" Featuring the Canberra Choral Society at the Canberra Theatre Centre, A.C.T.

The Canberra Choral Society originated in 1952 with a small group of people who began singing together for their own pleasure. It was conducted in its foundation years by Ronald Penny, Peter Baily and Jane Malone. The name was formalised in 1960 and the Society became officially incorporated in 1962. The history of the Society has been doscumented by Peter Campbell (Canberra PC Publishing 2002).

AND ... for her Canberra finale Ms Douglas produced -
"JAM, JELLY AND BREAD"
Production by SALT
Sponsored by Australia Council for the Arts
and described as a 3 - dimensional show.

Janet also took part in 3 Group Exhibitions in 1972, 1973 and 1974 at the Canberra Art Club Gallery - now the Canberra Art Workshop

"Artists from around Australia have been associated with The Canberra Art Club - including Max Meldrum, John Coburn, Clifton Pugh, John Bracks and Lloyd Rees.

The first annual exhibition was held at the Canberra University Cottage, featuring oil paintings by Max Meldrum — on sale for 150 guineas. The then National Art Gallery of NSW also lent Max Meldrum's painting PORTRAIT OF MY MOTHER for the exhibition.

In 1950, when the club's workshops and exhibitions were held in rooms in West Row at The Canberra University, it was granted 150 pounds from the Cultural Development Committee. At this point work started in earnest to shape, challenge and shake the city's contemporary art, beginning by bringing Margo Lewers and Allister Morrison from Sydney to show Canberra their abstract expressionist works in 1952.

The 1954 exhibition included 'hero' paintings by three of the then modernist gods of the Sydney art scene, Roland Wakelin, Margo Lewers and Jean Bellette.

The weaver Solvig Baas Becking, one of the first members of the club, invited prominent, forward-thinking artists from Sydney and beyond to give classes through the club in Canberra. Then during the 1950s and 1960s artists such as John Coburn and Clifton Pugh were brought to Canberra by the club to tutor members for six-week periods.

But, in the old days, the club never had a permanent home and was 'homeless' for several decades while city authorities only provided crumbs from their table to support their town's grass roots community art. This didn't deter the club members, though. They staged mini blockbuster art shows for the Canberra community.

The club itself, however, had to shift from venue to decrepit venue until each in turn was bulldozed for development. Often its studio homes were cold, draughty barracks-style huts abandoned after housing the city's early public service arrivals.

One of its homes was at Huts No. 7 and No. 8, at the ramshackle former Riverside hostel in the Kingston-Barton area — where the club hung 18 paintings from the Blake Prize. They included Donald Friend's ST JOHN and SCENES FROM THE APOCALYPSE, Eric Smith's PILATE WASHING HIS HANDS, and Lawrence Daws's GOLGOTHA– alongside two-metre tall wooden candlesticks from St Paul's Cathedral, London, and a cope and mitre lent by Bishop Burgmann.

The club lobbied for a National Art Gallery, appearing before the Senate Select Committee on the Development of Canberra in 1955. (The Australian National Gallery finally opened nearly 30 years later)".

History - The Canberra Art Club
and indeed the Australian National Gallery
Author : Unknown

During the period 1973 and 1974 Janey also took part in another 2 Group Exhibitions which were both held at The Civic Permanent Building Society, Canberra (aka Civic Co-operative Permanent Building Society).

By 1973 Janey's marriage was dissolving and she and her husband made the decision to separate. It was after the break up of her marriage that I first met Janey. I think she still lived in Canberra at Aranda, named after the Arrernte people of Central Australia and meaning "white cockatoo". With streets named for First Nation groups around Australia, the Occidental suburb of Aranda was the first built in 1967.

We met through two shared friends Stevie Dunstan the outstanding Melbourne electronics musician and John A.C. Darling (1946 - 2011) poet, filmmaker, Oxford and Canberran academic and the son of the then Chair of the Australian Broadcasting Commission, who like Janey became a Baliphile. Linda Buckingham, another Frensham student, and I met John on his very first visit to Bali in 1973 - he was there to connect with his then partner American writer, Madrone when, like nearly everyone, he fell in love with the island.

"Kevin Kearney noted in his diary ...

The car broke down again on 1 March, 1974 and Janey Douglas artist - sent a postcard

Silhouette of "Ethos", Civic Square
Canberra, A.C.T.
Have just come home from a week in Melbourne staying with Stevie.
The record has arrived!!! He has 500 copies of it under the grand piano in the living room. 497 now. Everyone sends their love.
Tons of love from us

KK received a copy of Dunstan's album along with a screen printed poster advertising the album on which Dunstan drew himself on the synthi with KK recording. The album was later stolen. The poster still exists."

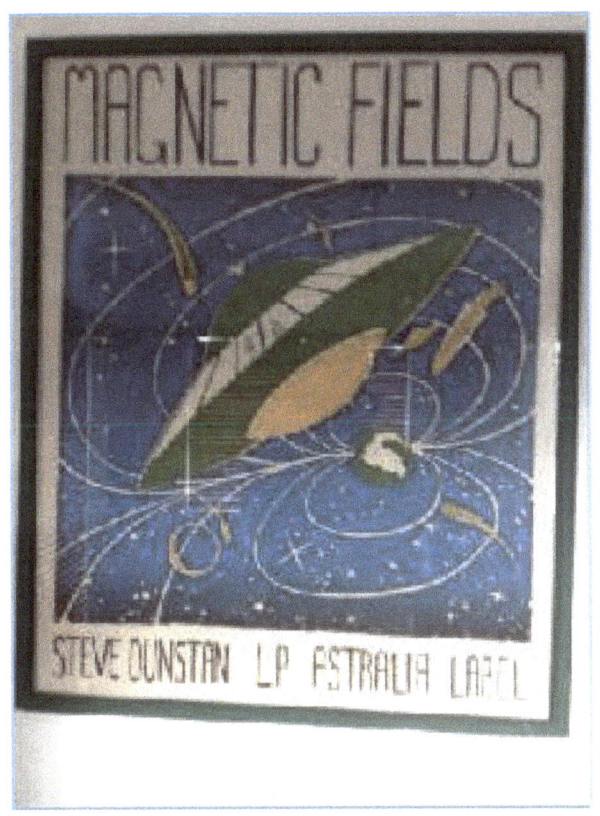

(Kevin J. Kearney, Sound Designer, Audio Artist, Analogue Location Sound Recordist, Vol 2 Part 1 : 2018, ISBN 978 1 387 65469 7 pp.200)

It was not long after our meeting in Canberra and Janey's trip to Melbourne that she relocated to Sydney and with her two daughters. Jessica and Miranda, moved to a house in Simmons Street, East Balmain. At the time Kevin and I were living on the corner of Simmons Street and Nicholson Street, East Balmain with Linda Buckingham and scenic artist Edward McCann

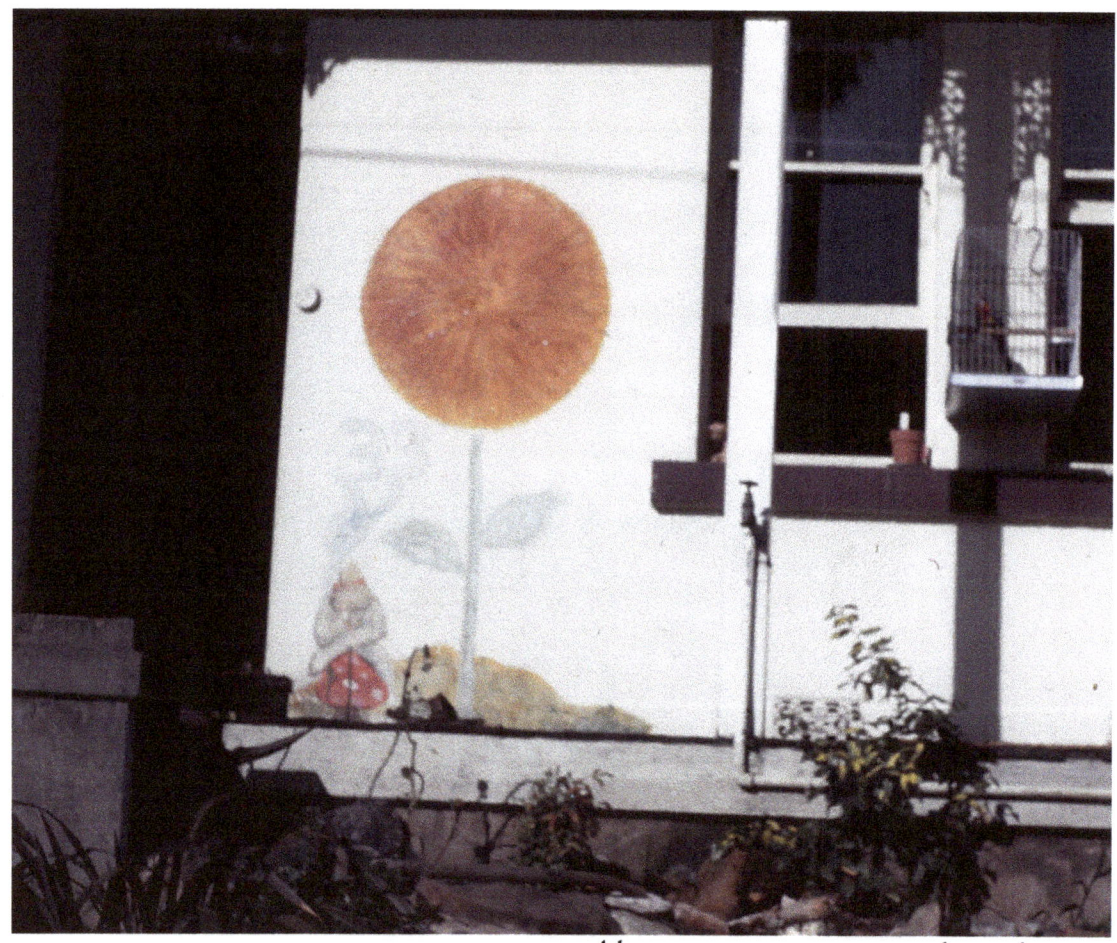

Mural by Scenic Artist : Edward McCann
Location : Front verahda
33 Nicholson Street, East Balmain
Still : Kevin J. Kearney (1936 - 2018)

I clearly remember the day that Janey visited for coffee and informed me that she was no longer Janey Douglas. She was taking a more feminist view of herself by reclaiming her own name - Janet Catherine Scott. And so it was from that time forward …

In May, 2022, Jessica Douglas remembering her move from Canberra to Balmain wrote :

"Nicholson St Public School was a revelation as a 10 year old, new in town. It was a small school in the 70s with two classes per classroom. Every morning our teacher (who was also the school's headmaster) used to bring out his piano accordion and we'd open up the #ABC songbook to start the day with Blue Suede Shoes or Good Morning Starshine and other classics of the day. He was rather eccentric, he looked like an accountant with a combover but he was a vegetarian, rowed on his rowing machine and taught us via index cards - self guided learning they'd call it today.

I suspect the headmaster role was demanding in a small school. We put on a production of #Oliver which blew my young impressionable mind. He also traveled in from Campbelltown each day which was a huge schlepp in the 70s. Mr Streetfield I salute you for helping to wake up my musical brain."

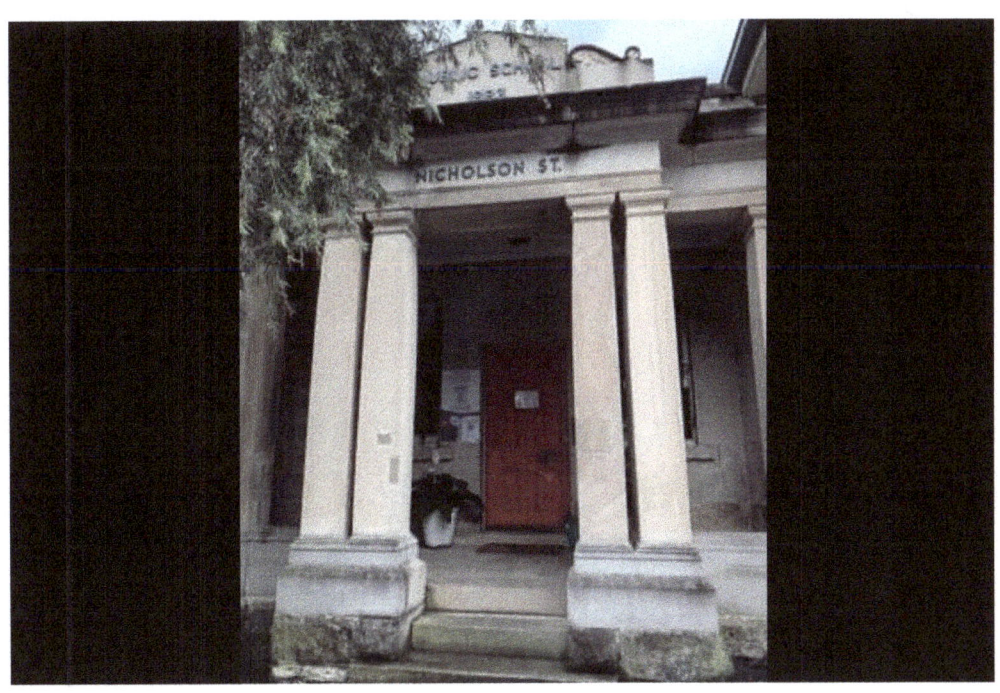

Entrance to Nicholson Street State School,
East Balmain

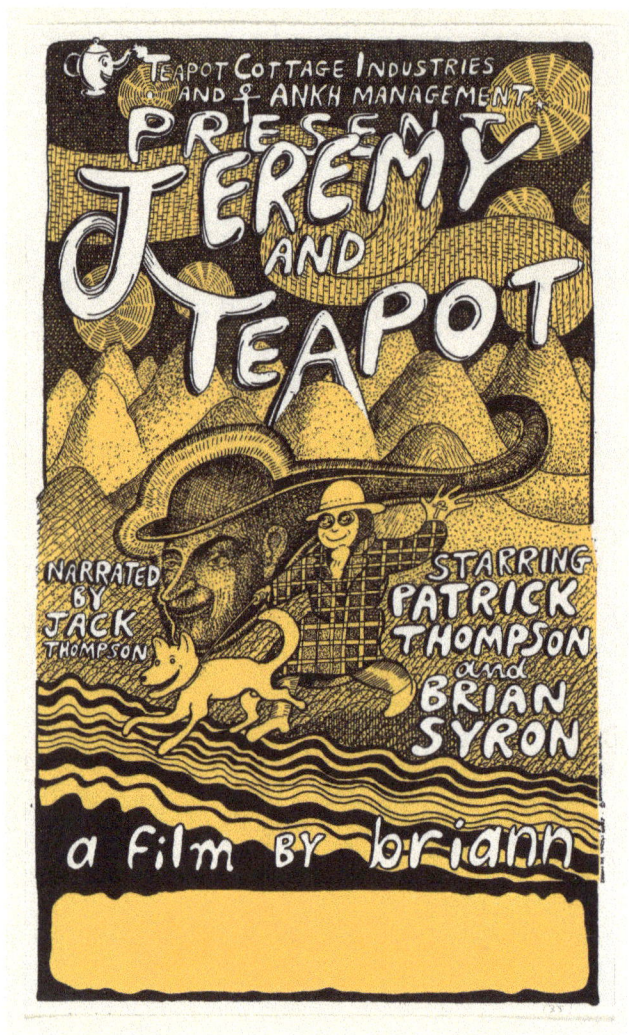

Mr. Streetfield was, indeed quite an amazing man because in 1975 he allowed his school choir to undertake composer/ musical director Stevie Dunstan's composition : MORNING STAR for the sound track of the short film JEREMY AND TEAPOT produced by Teapot Cottage Industries and Ankh Management, narrated by Jack Thompson, starring Brian Syron (1934 - 1993) and Patrick Thompson as well as featuring Jessica Douglas singing THE GRAND OLD DUKE OF YORK with actress Kris McQuade. The poster for the production was executed by artist Martin Sharp (1942 - 2013) and screen print artist Colin Little (1952 - 1982) founder of the Earthworks Poster Collective, Tin Shed, Sydney University.

Once Janet and her children were settled in East Balmain she almost immediately set to work cementing her place in the Sydney art scene and was invited to exhibit her work at Ace Bourke's new gallery.

Gallery   Ace's Art Shop
Gallery Owner / Curator   Ace Bourke
Location   144 Edgecliffe Rd., Woollahra

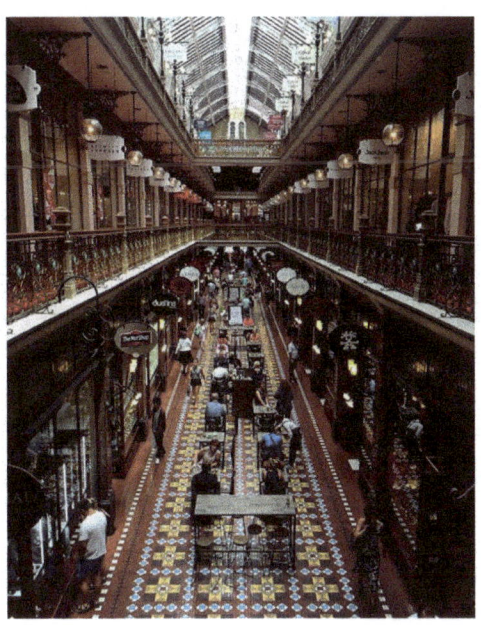

www.historyofsydney.com.au

I first met Ace through his very close friend John Darling when John stayed with Kevin and me on his return to Australia from Bali sometime in 1974. At the time Ace was running a palm and fern shop on the first floor of the Victorian style Strand Arcade, opposite Flamingo Park - the commercial outlet for Jenny Kee and Linda Jackson, at 195 - 197 Pitt Street, Sydney. I think Ace had not long arrived back in Australia from London where he and John Rendall were most famously known for their adoption from Harrod's of - "A Lion Called Christian".

The plant shop did not last long and so it was that in 1975 Ace opened ACE'S ART SHOP with its individually drawn calling cards by artists such as Peter Wright (1941-1999), Greg Weight, Peter Tully (1947 - 1992), Martin Sharp, Janet Scott and Stevie Dunstan and other recognised names. The gallery was based on the New York concept of a small shop front selling works of art with a kang in one corner where Bourke entertained and slept. In fact the shop was itself a piece of art.

Vogue Australia's description was :
"Sandwiched between a florist and a laundromat at 144 Edgecliff Road, Sydney is a refreshing new outlet for art works by some of Australia's most adventurous neorealist painters. Ace's Art Shop is just that - a shop not a gallery...But already four months old Ace's projects an exciting contemporary image. An image helped in infancy by the publicity attendant on purchases made by film star Jack Nicholson while he was in Sydney and the cabled order from Sammy Davis Jnr. (1925 -1990) in Hollywood for some electronic jewellery activated by tiny batteries by John Hansen. The little shop burgeons with attractive and amusing things from matchboxes hand painted by Steve Dunstan and pop paintings by Richard Liney ...Other artists include Martin Sharp and photographer Greg Weight.
                    "VOGUE AUSTRALIA - Art Showcases"

Janet's work on exhibition at Ace's Art Shop was very, very large crayon and pastel drawings of horses and Australian Rules players (among other things) and through Ace's Art Shop one of her paintings was acquired by Jack Nicholson in 1976 when he was in Sydney with Michael Douglas promoting his film ONE FLEW OVER THE CUCKOOS NEST (1975) and another of Janet's very, very large paintings was acquired by Sammy Davis Jnr..

During 1975 she was invited to hold a Solo Exhibition at the Hogarth Gallery.

QUADRANT (1975)

Medium :   Drawings
Date :   April, 1975
Location :   Hogarth Gallery
             7 Walker Lane, Paddington, Sydney
Director :   Clive Evatt Jnr. (1931 - 2018)

In his lifetime Clive Evatt was considered one of the best known defamation barristers in Sydney.   He represented many plaintiffs against media outlets including Harry Seidler, Abe Saffron and Gypsy Fire wrongly portrayed as Bob Dylan's "sex slave".   Mr. Evatt was struck off by the High Court in 1968 and took a 13 year lay off after he was found to have engaged in professional misconduct. He returned to the bar around 1981 with a greatly increased defamation practice.

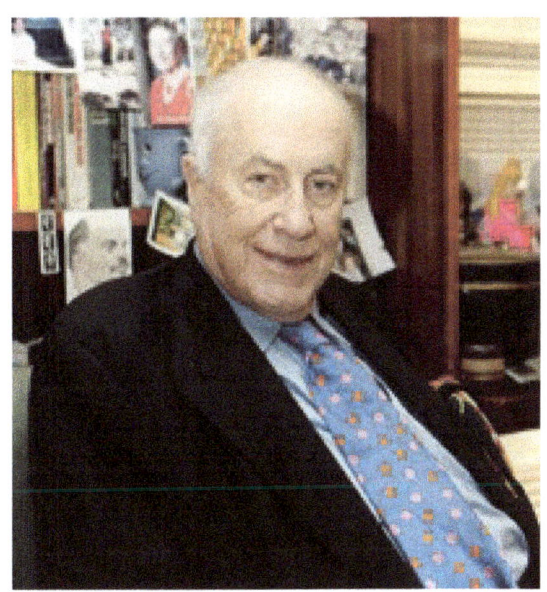

Clive Evatt Jnr. lawyer and art gallery owner

During his enforced break from practising at the Bar he became an art dealer, acquired a fine arts degree, amassed a valuable collection of art and set up the "pioneering Hogarth Galleries" in Paddington. NSW Bar Association president Arthur Moses, SC, described Mr. Evatt as "a renowned member of the NSW Bar, art collector and gallery owner".

Alan Spencer, who published the book JEREMY AND TEAPOT (1969) which was   illustrated in London in 1970 by artist Harriet Wheeler, was the winner of the $100,000 December, 1974 lottery. He flew out of Sydney to Hong Kong on April 29, 1975 and that evening Kevin and I caught a cab to Janet's QUADRANT exhibition at the Hogarth Gallery. Her exhibition was reviewed as follows :

"Janet Douglas is a new realist of the 70s with the nostalgia for the 30s and 40s which is so prevalent among the Australian younger generation of artists.   They seem to yearn for that period of the twentieth century immediately before they were born and their idols are the movie stars of the golden age of Hollywood and the heroes of the pre-World War II theatre and ballet.   Janet Douglas uses all the techniques and precision of the modern day realists but softens her images with a touch of romanticism so that her paintings evoke an emotional feeling of sympathy with the subject portrayed."

Sydney Morning Herald (date unknown)

"Leaving the Hogarth and catching a cab to Balmain for some reason Kevin found himself hobbling home to Birchgrove when he caught up again with his friend from the past, poet Shelton Lea (1946 - 2005). A very, very long night eventuated with him at "Teapot Cottage"...Early next morning Lea left Kearney with a roneoed copy of HAVE YOU EVER FELT SO LONELY THAT YOU HAD TO HUG A TREE - POEMS FROM A JAIL" inscribed - Thanks Kevin for a good, if strange, night."

(Ref. KJK, Audio Artist, Sound Designer & Analogue Location Sound Recordist - Vol. 2 Part 1 - pp.137 - 138)

Around November / December 1975 Scott undertook dance classes with British dance, actor and mime artist Lindsay Kemp (1938 - 2018) who was in Australia for his extraordinary performance as "Divine" in the outstanding stage production FLOWERS at the New Arts Theatre, Glebe Point Rd., Glebe. This exquisite production was freely based on Jean Genet's life with libretto and design by Kemp and music by Joje Hirota. Janet like many others was entranced and so studied with Kemp while he was available in Australia.

Then the next step in Scott's career path was the 1976 - 1978 study of photography at the Centre for Australian Photography (ACP). Originally conceived by leading Australian photographer David Moore it was officially founded in September, 1973 with an original committee that included the photographers David Moore, Wes Stacey and Laurence Le Guay among others. It is now recognised as one of Australia's oldest contemporary arts organisation.

"The ACP holds at its core the vital contribution of artists and photographers in distilling and reflecting upon society, displaying a pluralism of perspectives and a breadth of artistic practice."
                    About Us - Australian Centre for Photography

Ever busy, Janet taught at the Willoughby Art Centre, Willoughby during 1976 and 1977. This Centre established in 1961 by Joy Ewart (1916 - 1964) is an arts hub and community driven resource supporting artists and helping people of all ages to participate in the arts, supported by local artists and the community to promote an appreciation of the creative and visual arts.

During the course of study and teaching, Scott undertook the purchase of the corner shop in Birchgrove and in June, 1976 I visited with Janet at her home on the Cnr. of Grove Street in Birchgrove to meet up with shared old friends, Jinta and her husband, artist Gerhard

25

Viet, from Gymea Bay and Bali who were now living at Nullum Forest in northern N.S.W.

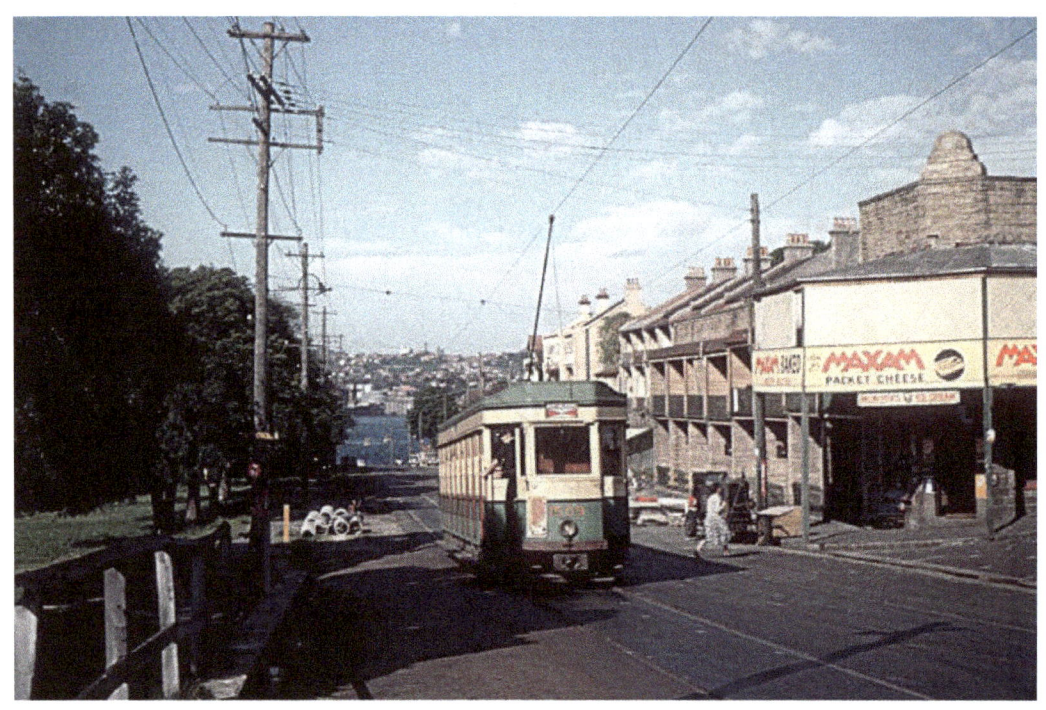

In the olden days the Birchgrove tram services branched off from the main line on Darling Street, turning left into Rowntree Street, then another left into Cameron Street, before turning right into Grove Street and finishing at Wharf Road, Birchgrove. Services terminated in 1954. This is a very early photograph taken 20 years prior to Janet acquiring her property (the corner shop) in 1974. but the shop looked much like this when Janet moved in.

At this time Janet took part in two Group Exhibitions one in 1976 another in 1977.

1. "WOMEN IN SOCIETY" (1976)
Gallery   The Hogarth Gallery
Jude Adams writing about this exhibition for the University of Western Australia in her article OUTSKIRTS - Feminisms along the edge - LOOKING FROM WITH/IN FEMINIST ART PROJECTS OF THE 70s and specifically "Sydney WAM 1974 - 1977" says :

"I was fortunate enough to meet (Ann) Newmarch OAM (1945 - 2022) the following year when we both had work in the exhibition IT'S GREAT TO BE AN AUSTRALIAN WOMAN, Hogarth Gallery (Nov 1975). Hogarth Gallery included a follow up exhibition in 1976 WOMEN IN SOCIETY ...."

It was in this second exhibition that Janet, a very early advocate for the equal opportunity of women to be recognised in the artistic milieu, exhibited her work. Unfortunately there is, again, little information about this exhibition although I suspect that Janet would have agreed with Ann Newmarch who, after holding her first solo exhibition at the Robert Bolton Gallery in Adelaide, criticised commercial galleries for being dominated by male artists and driven by the market and even though Sydney Women's Art Movement (WAM) folded in 1976 it did rise again in various other guises at a later date.

2. "APOCALYPSE: (1977)
Gallery   The Hogarth Gallery
I have no futher details regarding this particular exhibition.

Janet worked on a short feature in 1978 for Teapot Cottage Industries :

AND / OR = ONE (1982)
Pre-production Photographer/
Poster Artist   Janet Scott
Location :   Beryl Larkin's White Studio,
                                 Ocean Street, Woollahra
Hair & Makeup Designer   Irene Walls
Cast: Kris McQuade, Anna West, Bridget Murphy

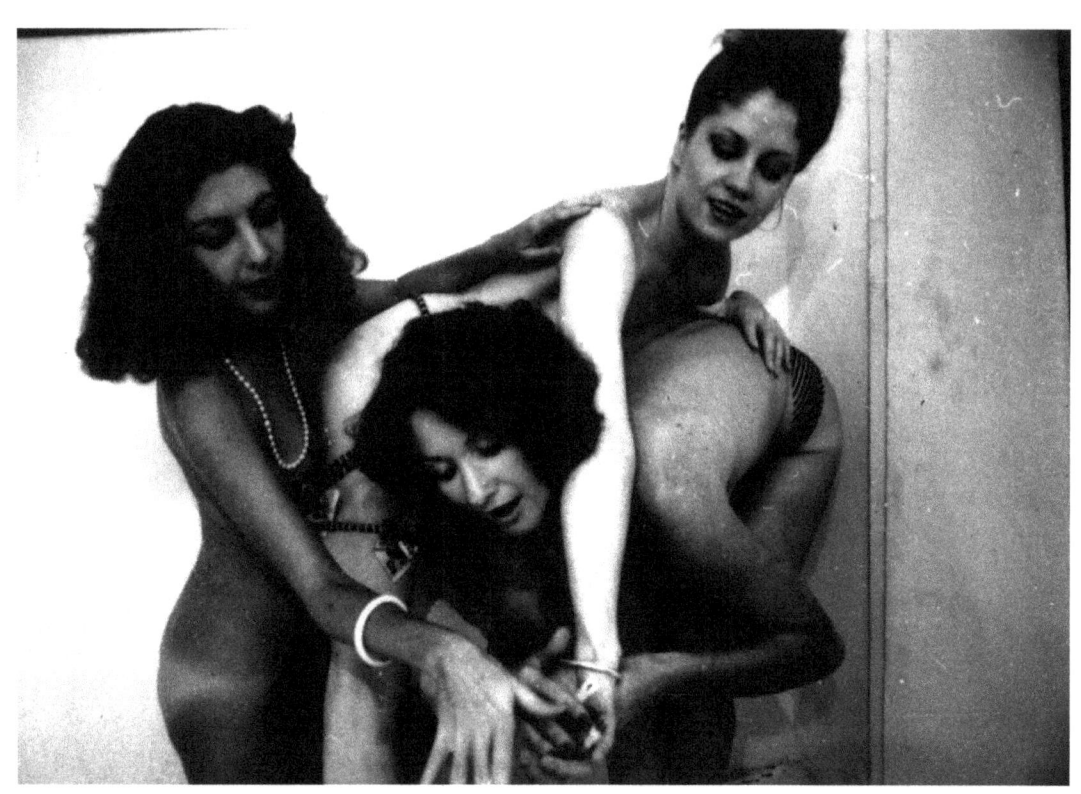

'THE CAST" (1977)
Photographer : Janet Scott
L to R : Anna West / Kris McQuade / Bridget Murphy

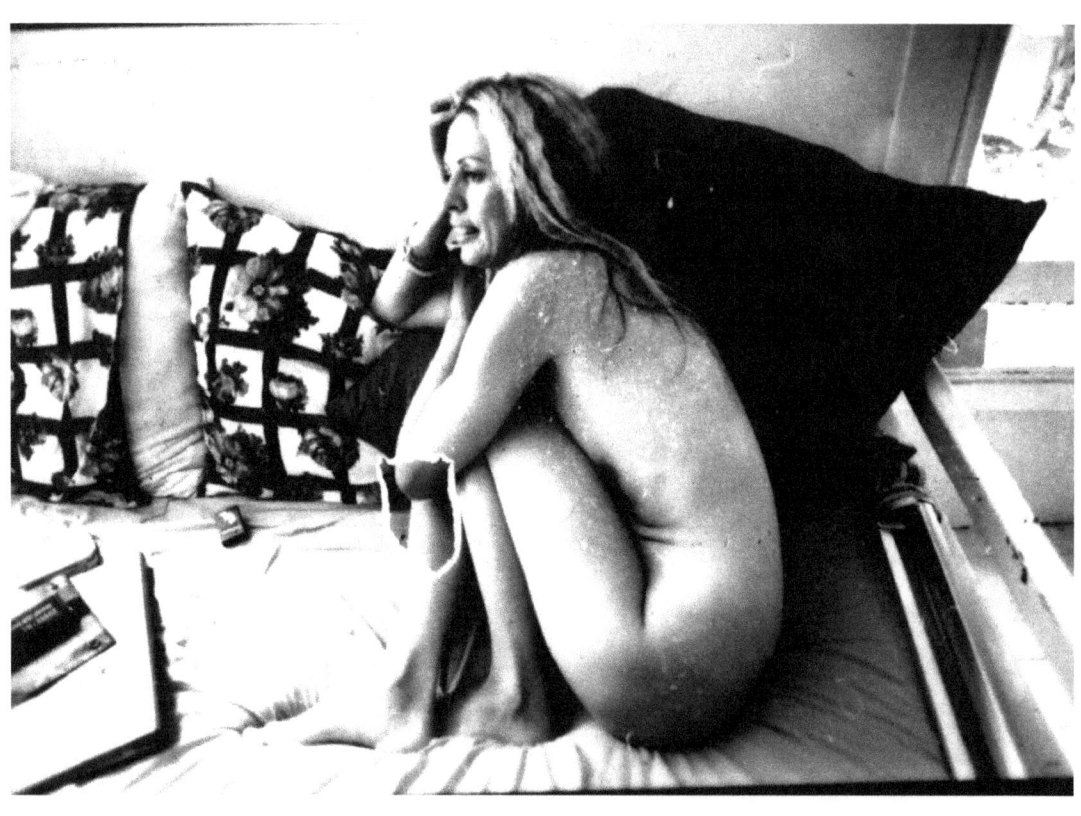

"THE DIRECTOR" (1977)
Photographer : Janet Scott

28

Around this time Janet began taking photographs of family and friends to use at a later date.

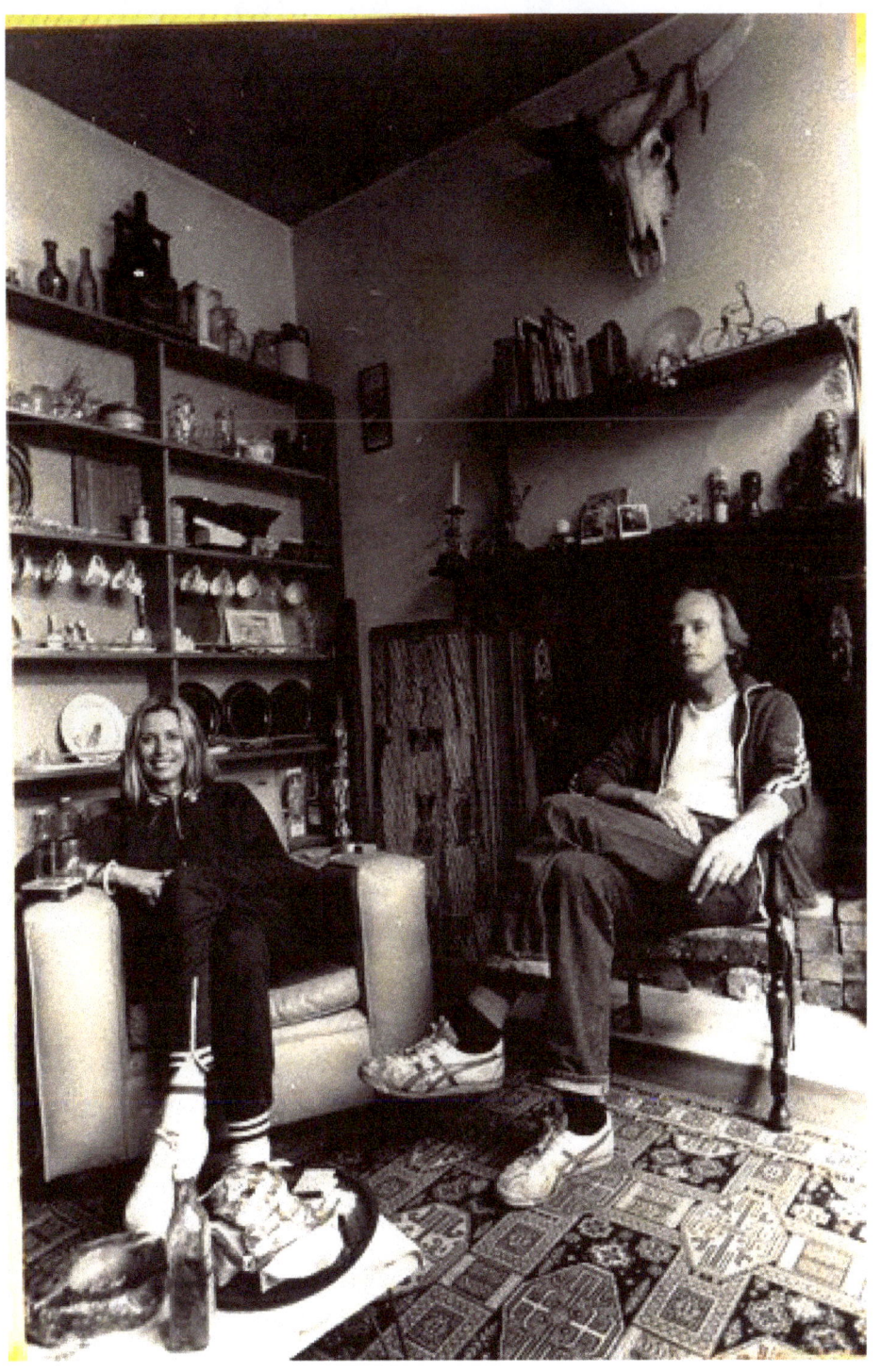

"KEVIN & BRIANN" (1978)
Photographer : Janet Scott
"Teapot Cottage"
21 Gipps Street, Birchgrove

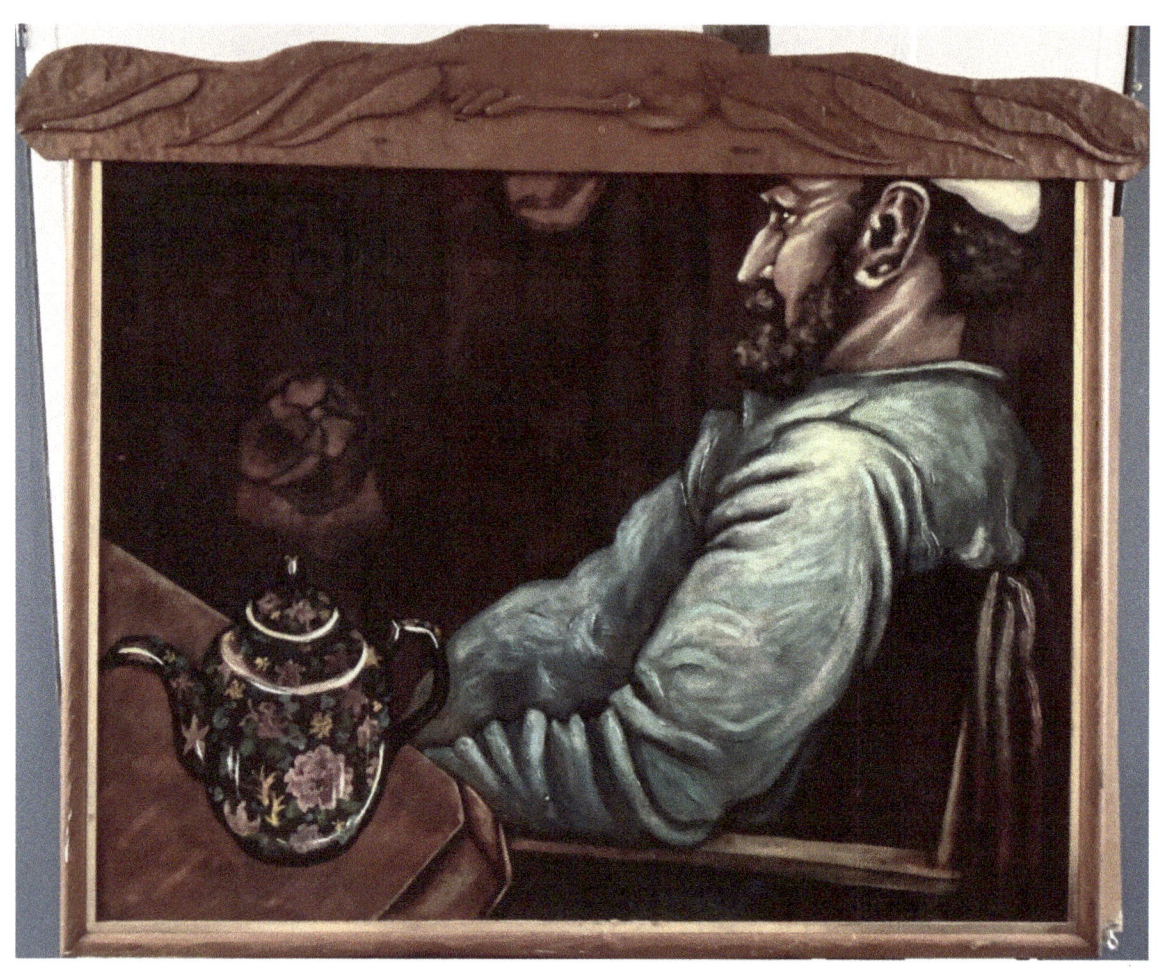

"ADRIAN ~ AT MY TABLE" (1978)
Artist ~ Janet Scott
Carved Wooden Frame ~ Janet Scott

Adrian Rawlins (1939 ~ 2001) was one of Janet's coterie of good friends who was a frequent visitor to STUDIO FACADE and who also became one of her portraits.

"Adrian grew up in a Jewish household in Caulfield and St. Kilda , studied theatre with Frank Thring, was an ardent Bob Dylan fan for almost all his life and moved into running the FAT BLACK PUSSYCAT a contemporary and experimental jazz venue in Melbourne. He became a poet, performer and promoter, both of himself and bands such as the Red Onions who later became the LOVED ONES with among other band members, Kim Lynch, who I first met in 1968 when he moved to Paddington, Sydney from Melbourne with his partner, Maori princess Nu. They worked at J.Walter Thompson's before moving to England where, Kevin and I stayed with them in Little Venice, London and Inverness Scotland. Rawlins moved to Sydney around the same time as Kim and fell under the spell of the mystic poet and musician Nevill Drury who I met when KJ worked on the documentary THE OCCULT EXPERIENCE (1985) scripted by Mr. Drury, filmed around the world and cited as "the result of 12 years research by internationally recognised expert on the occult, Nevill Drury..."

In 1969 Adrian worked with the producer of the OURIMBAH POP FESTIVAL Maureen Phillips (aka Pilgrimage For Pop). He also made a major audience appearance in Gordon Mutch's experimental documentary about the Ourimbah Festival (among other things) - ONCE AROUND THE SUN (which was finally edited and completed by David Huggett in 2012). FESTIVALS IN AUSTRALIA - AN INTIMATE HISTORY was published in 1986 and both Janet and I have copies of this almost hand made booklet. He also read his poetry in the film JOHN OLSEN : JOURNEY THROUGH "YOU BEAUT" COUNTRY (1992) when John Olsen takes the viewer "on an Australian journey through his own eyes and the paintings of his friends including Donald Friend (1915 - 1989), Lloyd Rees (1895 - 1988), Jeffrey Smart (1921 - 2013), Clifton Pugh (1924 - 1990), Tim Storrier and Margaret Olley (1923 - 2011)" to name a few.

As well as Janet's portrait of Adrian there is a startling life-sized sculpture of him by Peter Corlett called THE LAUGHING POET sitting atop a column in Brunswick Street, Fitzroy where he used to sell audiotapes of himself reciting Shakespeare's sonnets ... of which, again, both Janet and I have copies. He was, like Janet, a true eccentric and they were never boring.

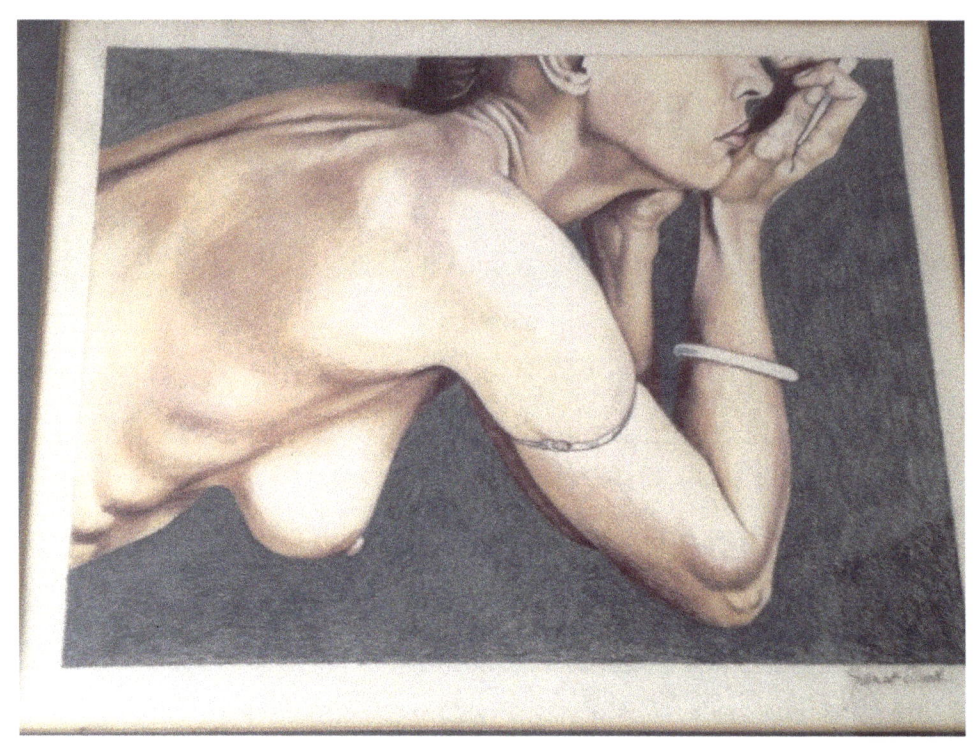

BRIANN - 1 (1979)
Artist :   Janet Scott
Medium :   Pastel on paper

NEW FACES (1979)
Gallery   Robin Gibson Gallery
Gallery Owner / Curator   Robin Gibson
Location   44 Gurner St.,
                                 Paddington, N.S.W.
Date   25 August. 1979

Janet was invited and took part in the Group Exhibition NEW FACES and exhibited 2 x coloured pastel nude drawings on paper titled (I think) : BRIANN 1 and BRIANN 2 by Janet Scott at Robin Gibson Gallery.

Mr. Gibson's elegant gallery was established in 1976 and ART Investor advises that "the gallery is known for its eclectic stable of artists - including established, emerging, traditional, modernist, contemporary and outsider - with a focus on painting and sculpture.

The gallery focuses on living Australian artists including (currently) Guy Gilmour, Andrew Hopkins and Zoe Tweedale but the gallery also represents a number of Artists Estates" including such artists as :

American / Australian sculptor Clement Meadmore (1929 - 2005), American based Australian artist Ann Wienholt (1920 - 2018) who was "concerned with capturing the curious, strange and wonderful."
South American born / Australian artist Bryan Westwood (1930 - 2000) who won the Archibald Prize twice - once with a portrait of Prime Minister Paul Keating and then with a portrait of Elwyn Lynn.
and
Elwyn Lynn (1917 - 1997) an Australian artist, author, critic at The Australian and curator of the Power Gallery of Contemporary Art at Sydney University from 1969 - 1983.

I was fortunate enough to speak with Mr. Gibson on 6 May, 2022 when I phoned to find out the original address of the Robin Gibson Gallery and surprisingly Mr. Gibson answered the phone. I told him that I was compiling this little book about Janet Scott who had exhibited at his gallery some 43 years previously and he immediately replied ... "Janet from Balmain".   He advised me that he was no longer located at the above address but, amazingly and wonderfully, he remembered "Janet from Balmain".   I thought how remarkable is that considering the number of artist that Mr. Gibson would have been involved with in all those years ... It seemed to give "JANET SCOTT .. Artist" an extra fillip.

In 1979 Janet painted the film poster
 AND / OR = ONE (1982)
Medium   Pencil on Paper

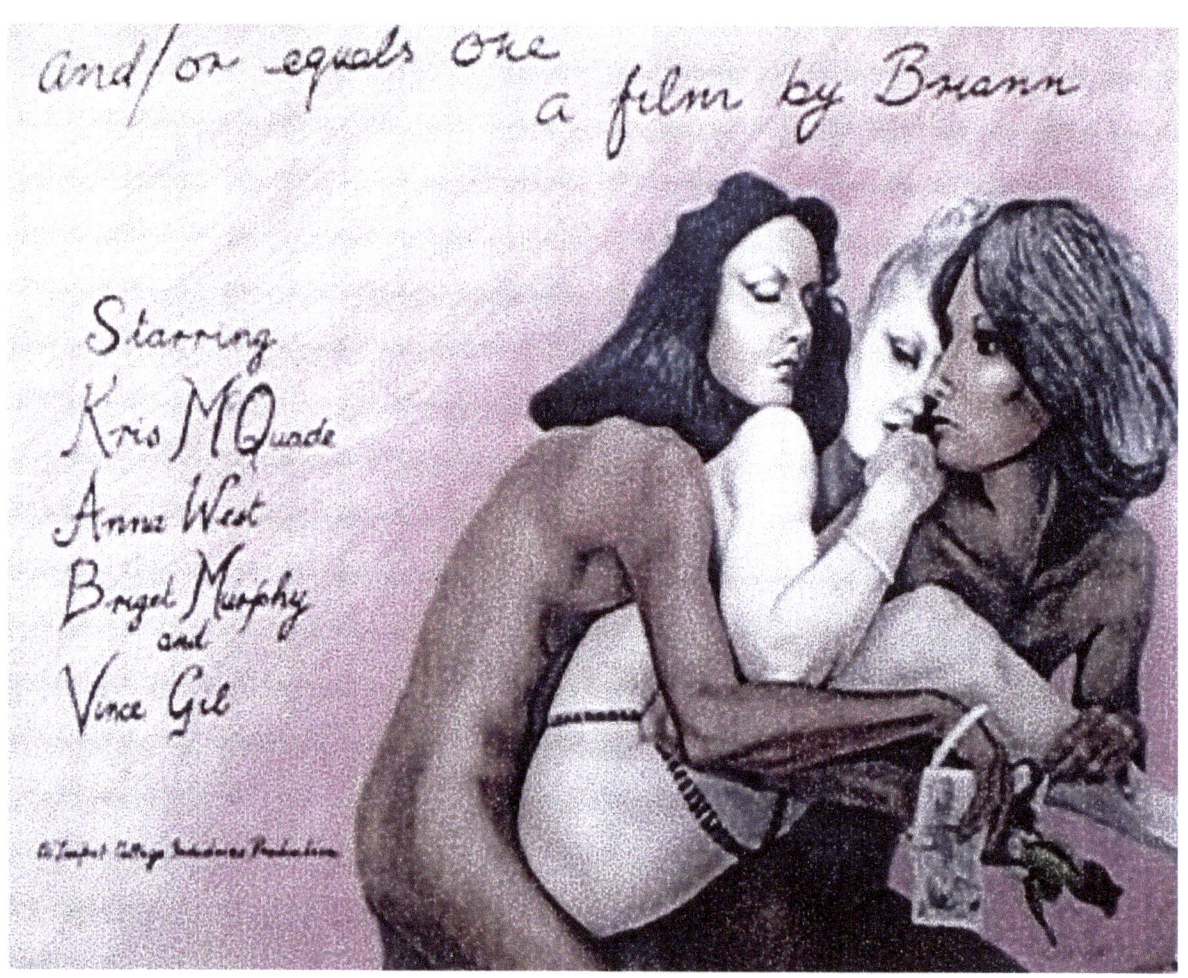

Artist : Janet Scott

L to R ~ Anna West, Bridget Murphy, Kris McQuade

On completion Janet delivered her poster for AND / OR = ONE to "Teapot Cottage" 21 Gipps St., Birchgrove.

Among its many screenings AND / OR = ONE (1982) was invited to and nominated Best Film @ the 1984 Women's Film & Video Festival, Tucson, Arizona, U.S.A.

Some time later Janet asked Irene Walls and myself to take part in a photographic shoot so that she could use the photographs in some way towards her next exhibition although at the time she was not sure what one that would be. The photographic shoot was held in Irene's studio in King St., Balmain.

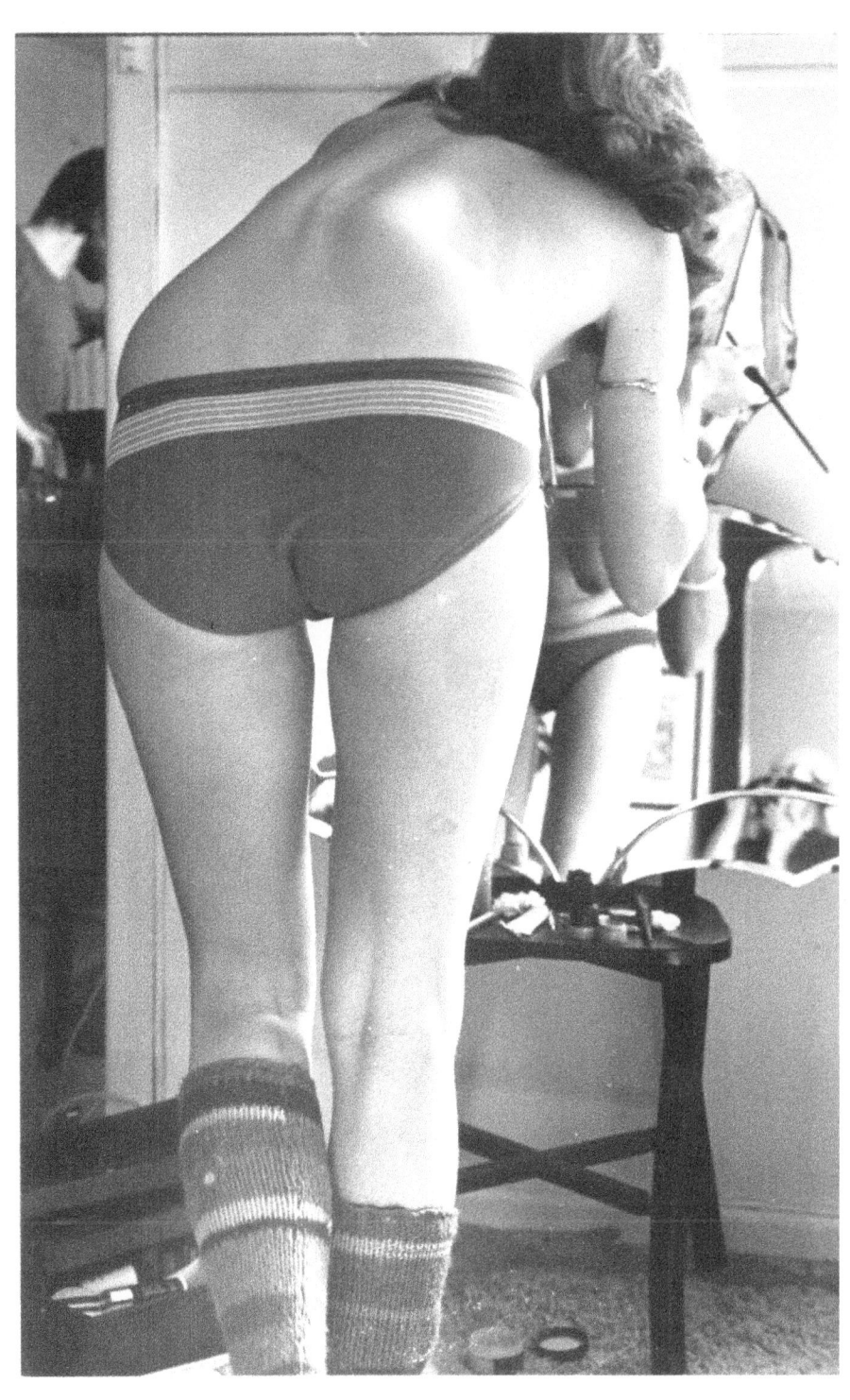

"GETTING READY (1979)
Photographer : Janet Scott
Location : Studio, King St., Balmain
This print belonged to Thomas G. Donovan, (1928 - 2016)
U.S.A. writer / executive producer
L.A., Ca., Kahala, Hi. and Palm Beach, Fla.

SUNDAY
at
15 CAMPBELL ST., BALMAIN
&
STUDIO FACADE, Cnr. GROVE ST., BIRCHGROVE

Visited friends today - Digby first
We sat in the sleep out
Discussed world affairs -
The thrill of knowing someone
who made it at Cannes -
The latest average income -
Bought a deal -
Talked about why feminists all look the same
Digby spent a great night with a roomful of feminists
"All feminists - you could tell!" Well …. nearly all.

Visited Janet next -
Nobody home, except Mandy.
Took the film upstairs
Walking through a wonder world of things
Casually sprawled across the rooms.
Around the studio - paintings, photographs, writing
Glass objects before glass refracted the sunlight
Latticed shadows quietly stilled my mind.
Recharged I continued on through Sunday.

"Blakeville"
104 Foucart St., Rozelle
24.5.1980
"FRAGMENTS OF ACID & REMNANTS OF LOVE"
1st Edition (1983) 1 of 1 - Private Publication
3rd edition 2021 - ISBN 078 1 4477 0260 4 p.32

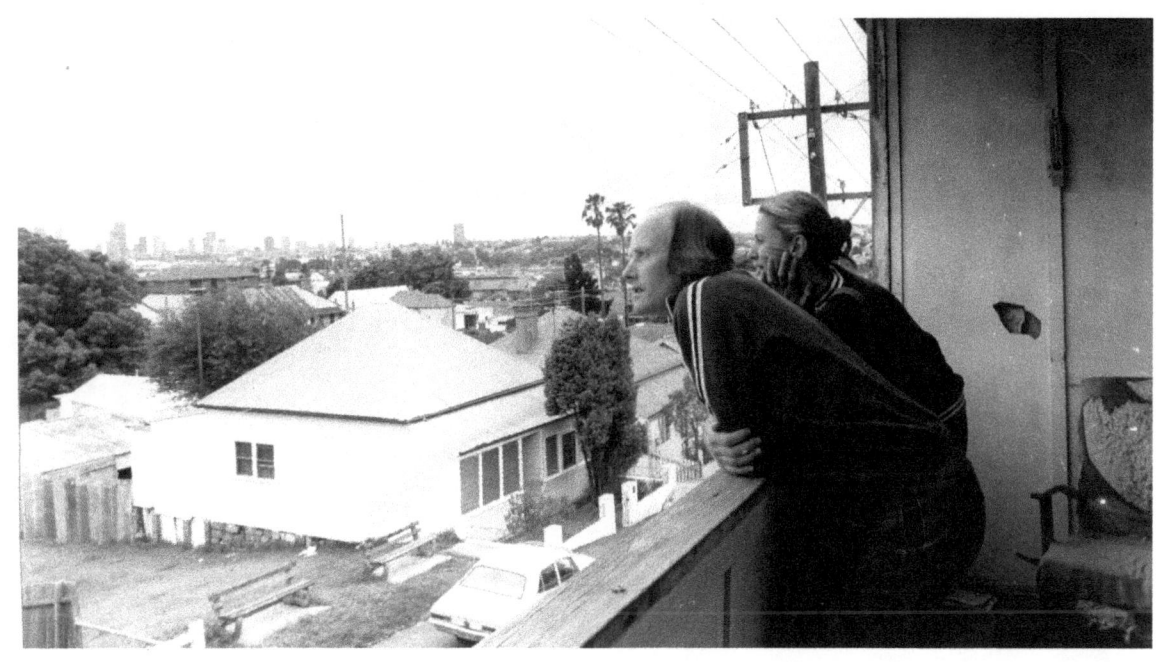

"ADMIRING THE VIEW (1980)
Photographer : Janet Scott
Before the renovations
"Blakeville"
104 Foucart St., ROZELLE

This shoot was the base for Janet's painting EMOH WEN RUO (1983)

Then it was in 1980 that Janet took the next step and as the founder formally opened the first art gallery in Birchgrove

STUDIO FACADE
Cnr. Grove and Bay Sts.
Birchgrove
"A small gallery in search of a sense of humour"

She opened up the top floor of the building with lattice and it became her studio and she made the ground floor shop area into "STUDIO FACADE" - the art gallery and in the almost 5 years of Janet's curatorship many national and international artists, including herself, were exhibited by Janet.

After the flurry of activity moving, setting up the gallery and doing minor home renovations Janet took a well earned vacation in Bali where she spent the months of April and May, 1980 falling in love.

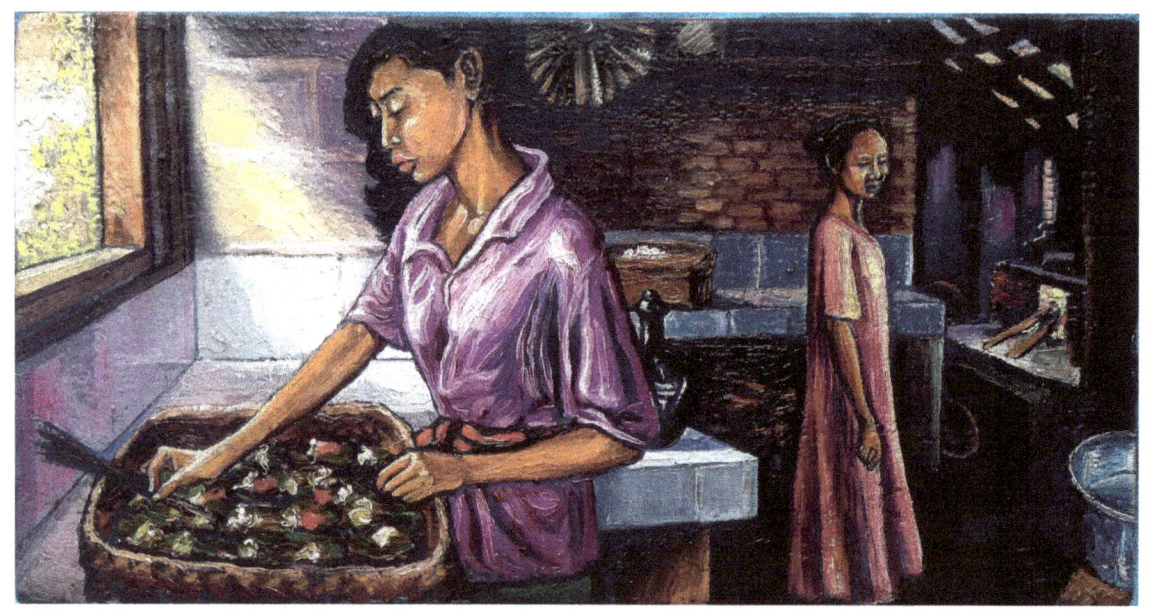

"MAKING JAJANS AT THE LOSMEN (1980)

Artist :   Janet Scott

In 1981 Janet's third child, a beautiful Australian / Balinese daughter Akea Scott was born at home on 15 January with loving family and friends to support Janet and to welcome Akea into the world. From that moment I suspect life became increasingly hectic but Janet, as always, sallied forth.

On 25 April, 1981 there was a formal opening of the Gallery with an exhibition of Janet's own works.

Almost concurrently Ms Scott was invited to exhibit her work in a Group Exhibition celebrating the Albury Regional Gallery's opening on 29 June, 1981 by N.S.W. Premier Neville Wran in the city's former Town Hall. The first director of the Gallery, Audray Banfield, set the focus on the museum's collection as photography and regional artists with a national reputation.

The Gallery is now known as the Murray Art Museum Albury (MAMA) and is a contemporaru art museum still located in Albury, N.S.W.

The Inaugural opening of STUDIO FACADE's first themed exhibition took place on 4 July, 1981 at the gallery's Birchgrove, Sydney location with THE FANTASTIC FUNNY 4TH JULY SHOW 1981. This was an invitation exhibition to Janet's many friends to exhibit and sell their work and a crowded night it was …

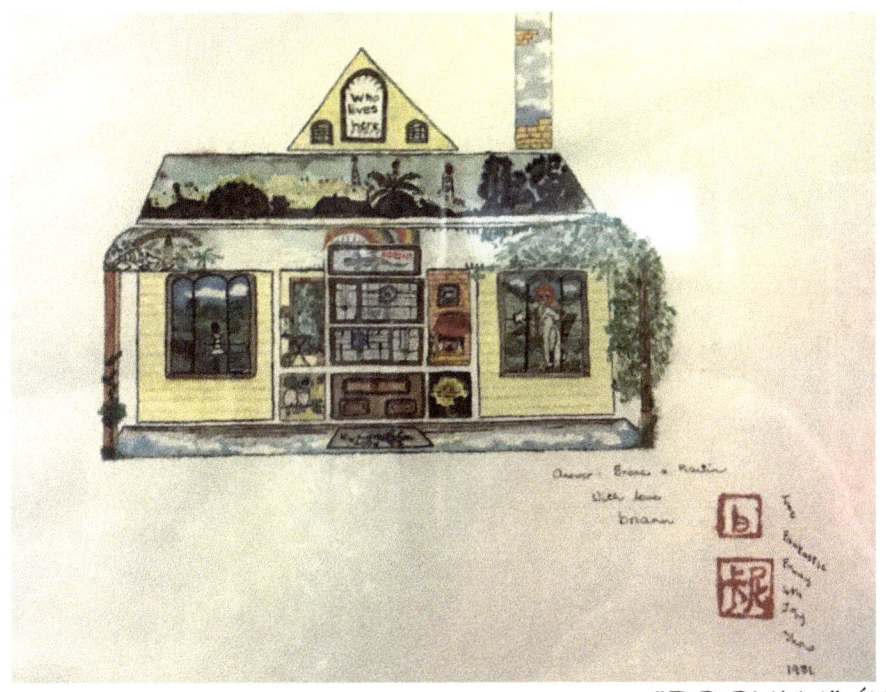

"POOYAM" (1981)
The Studio, King St., Balmain
Artist :   briann
Photograph of painting : Irene Walls

Recognised artists included Jane Le Rossignol musician, illustrator, painter and animation artist who throughout the years painted several vistas of actor Jack Thompson AO's properties.   Steve Dunstan who exhibited his matchbox paintings of ships. Ken Beatty Sculptor and installation artist whose company "Ploisons" made inflatible sculptures for PACT, UBU and the Mildura Sculpture Triennial and who exhibited his "GREAT WHITE SHARK". Irene Walls makeup artist, hair stylist and sculptress whose credits included DR. WHO (from 1966 - 1969) chose to include "THE FLYING DICK" (1981) which was quite a sensation. I submitted my "POOYAM" (1981) a little painting of Irene's King St., Balmain studio which forms part of my own matchbox art collection although I don't own the painting anymore . It was a thrill for all especially me to see my own work in an art gallery. Thank you Janet. Exhibitions now took place on a regular basis but I can only find some

13.12.1981   IMMACULATE CONCEPTION EXHIBITION
of which I have no further information.

In 1982 Janet and her family made a trip to Canada and the U.S.A. when Janet was invited to exhibit at the Bellair Gallery, Toronto, Canada which in the 1960s was located in Toronto's bohemian cultural centre considered "the breeding ground for some of Canada's most noted musical talents including Joni Mitchell, Neil Young and Gordon Lightfoot as well as then-underground literary figures such as Margaret Atwood, Gwendolyn MacEwen and Dennis Lee." Not surprisingly, by the 1980s real estate values had increased and the area became one of high end retail including many art galleries, fashion boutiques and antique dealers.

While she was there Janet also included her work in the 1982 International Women's Day Fair (Toronto) which in 1982 Canada was focused on a strategy to get more government funding and action for day care. I suspect an issue that Janet as a mother of three, especially as a mother of a very young child, would have strongly supported.

Returning refreshed from her visit to North America Janet set to work in 1982 to co-found the inner city "artists' co-operative" ANTARES GALLERY. and began work towards the first showing of the community group's work.

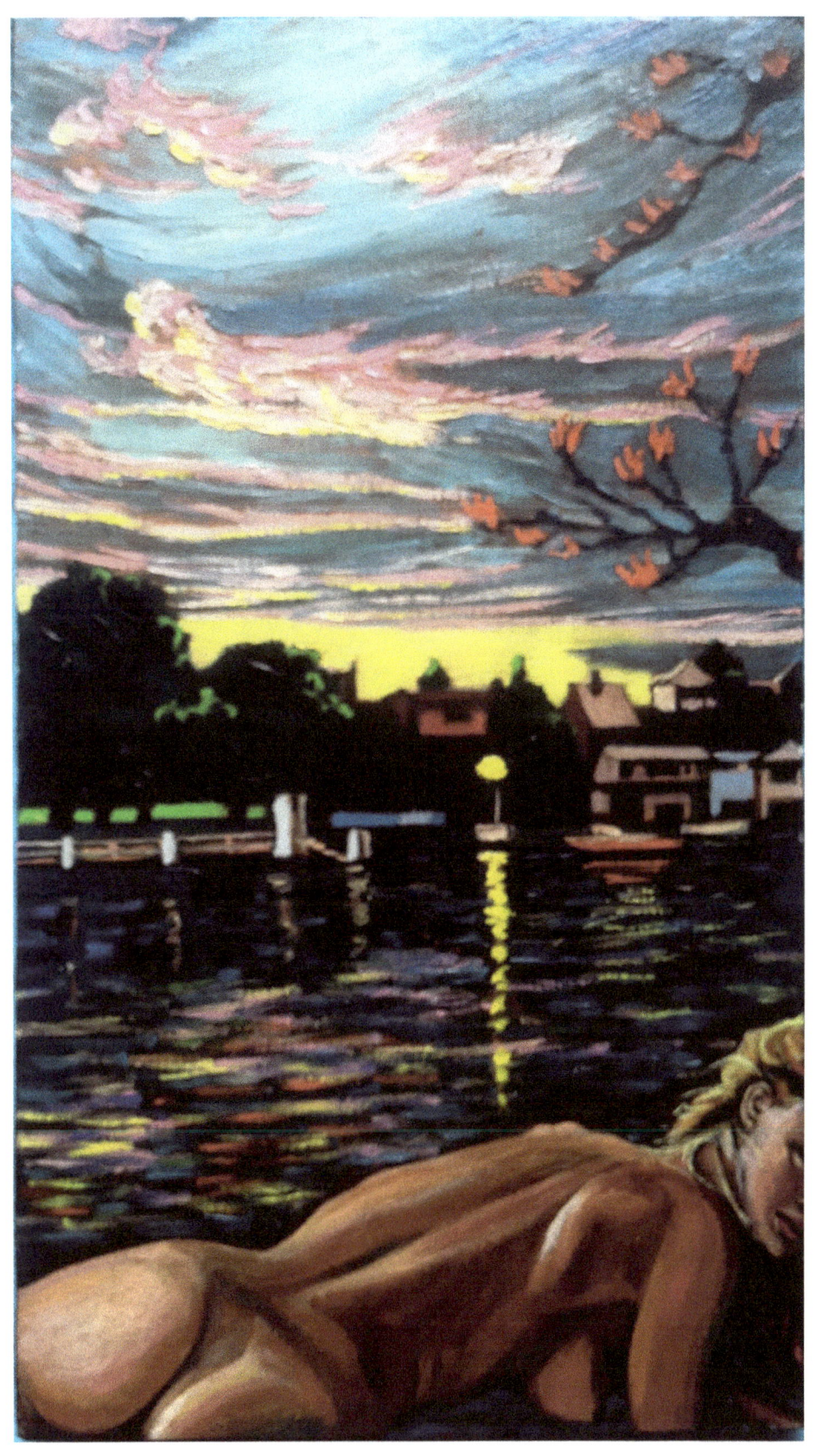

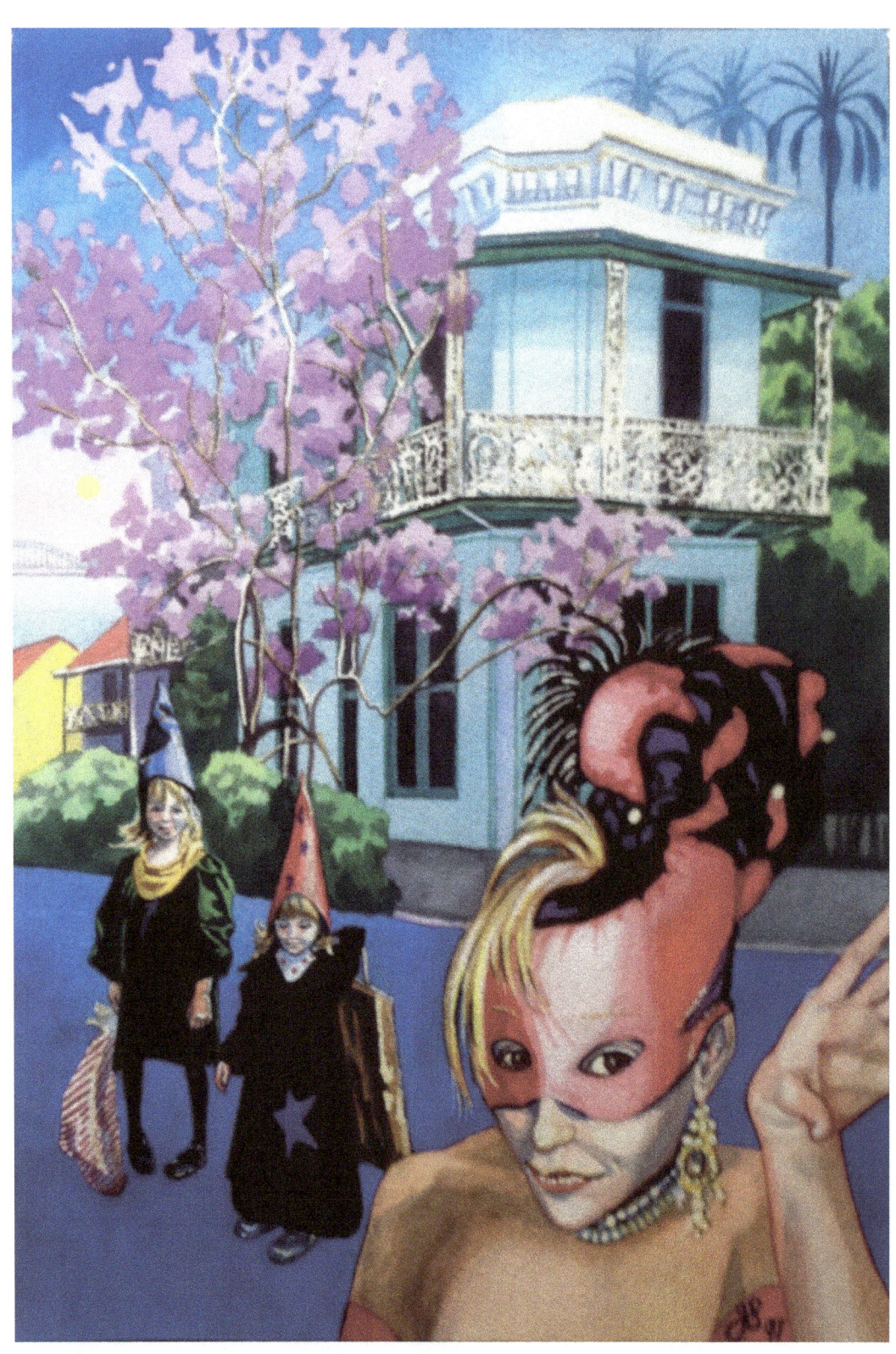

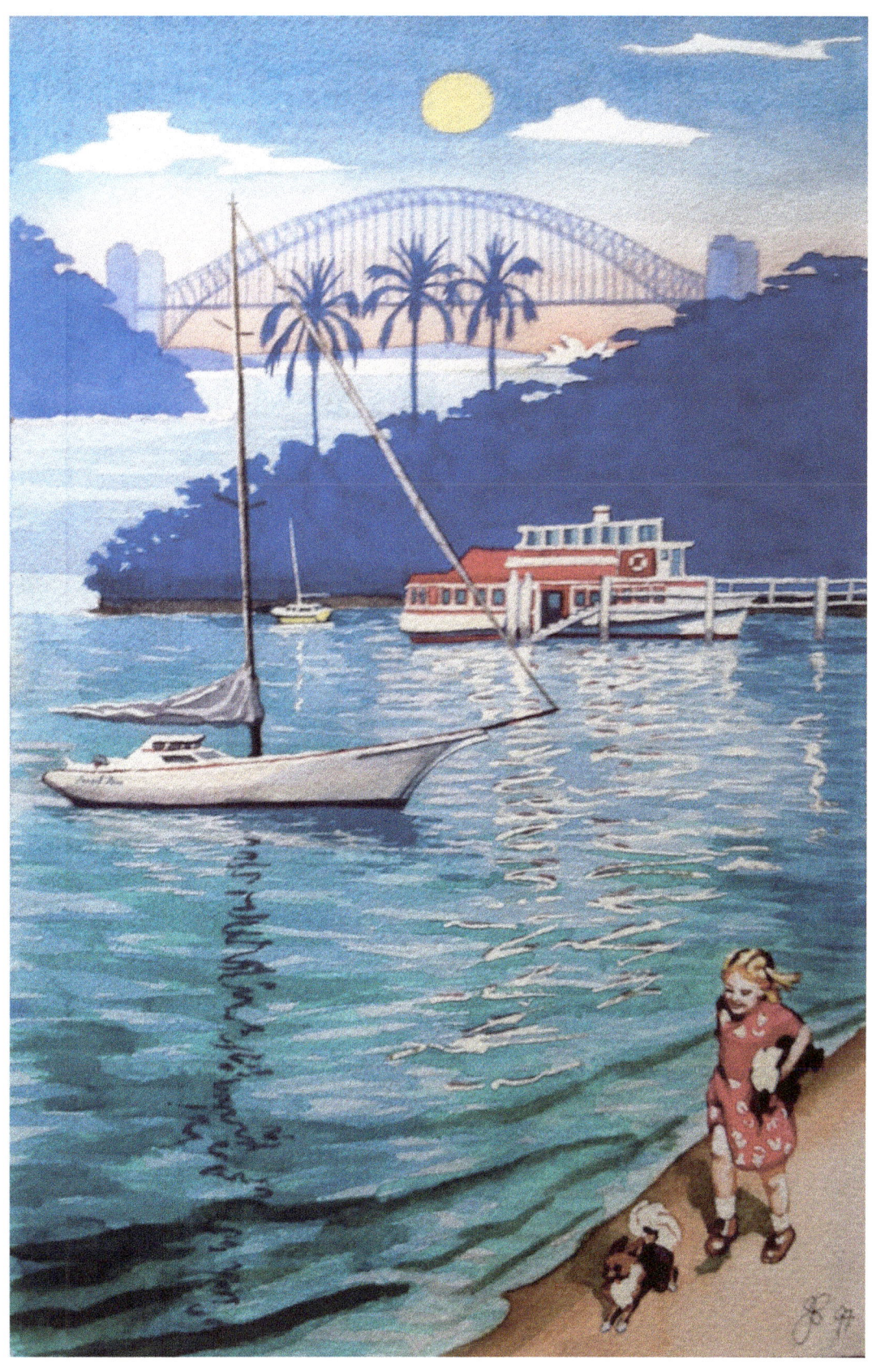

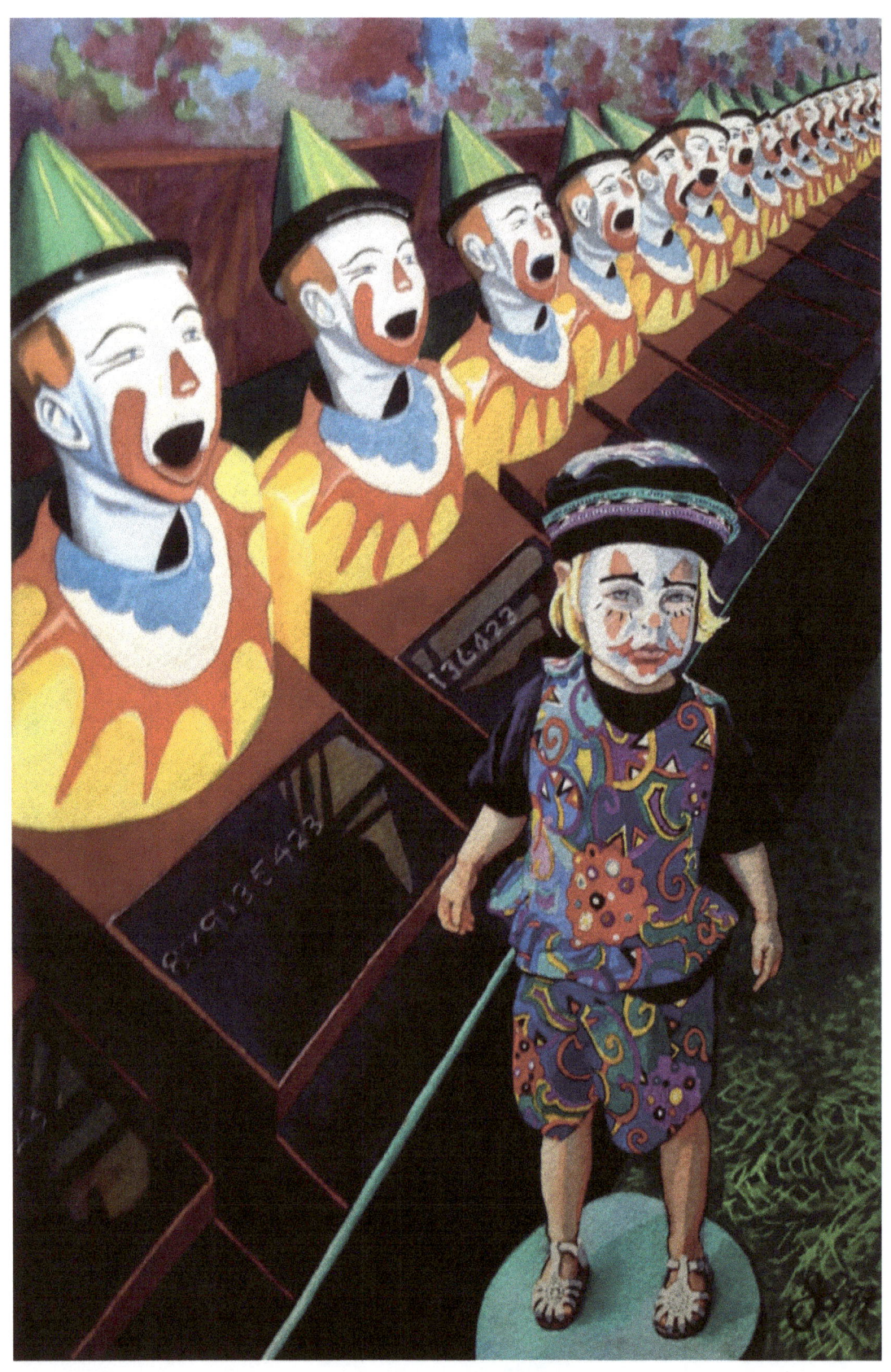

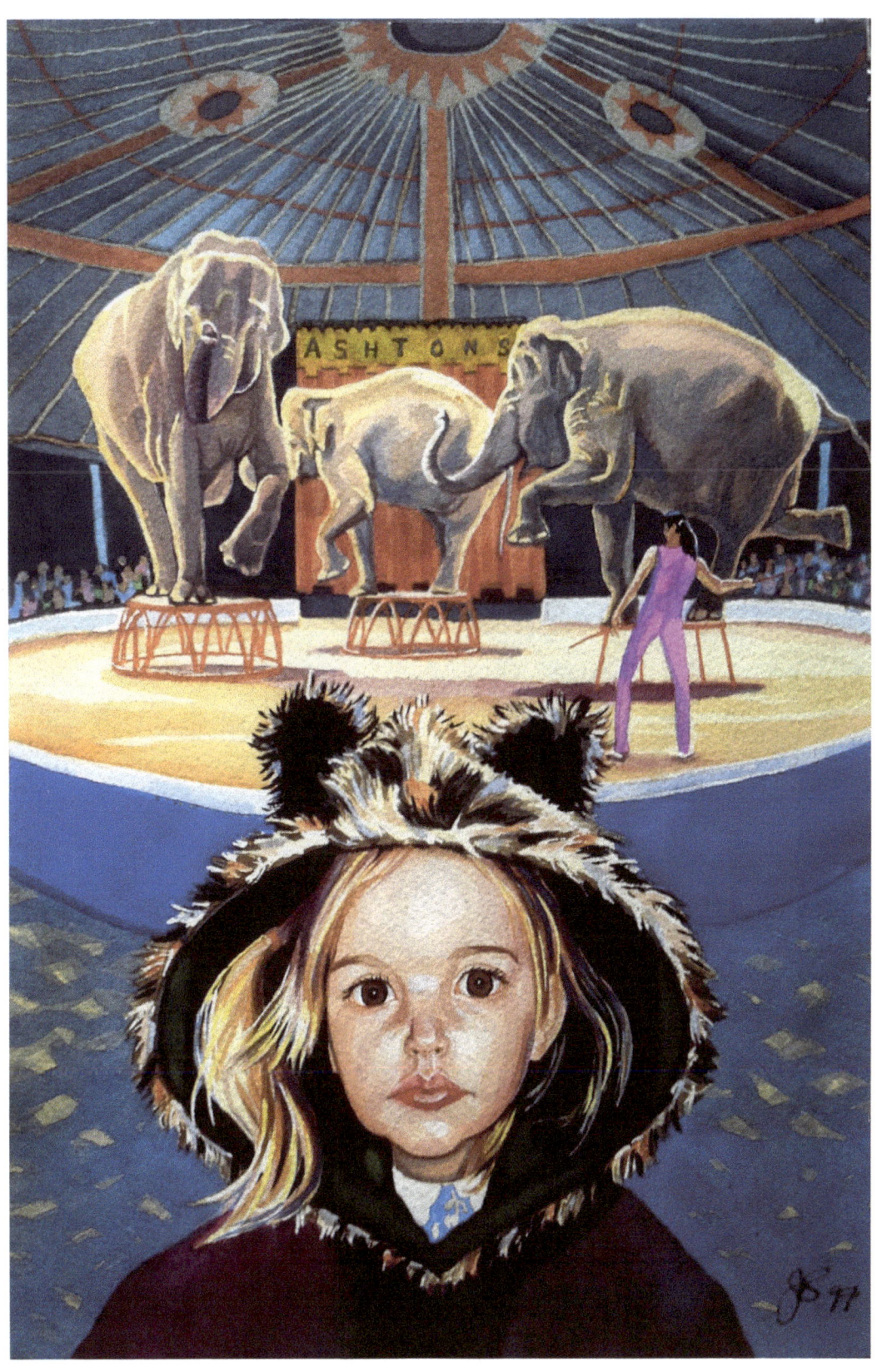

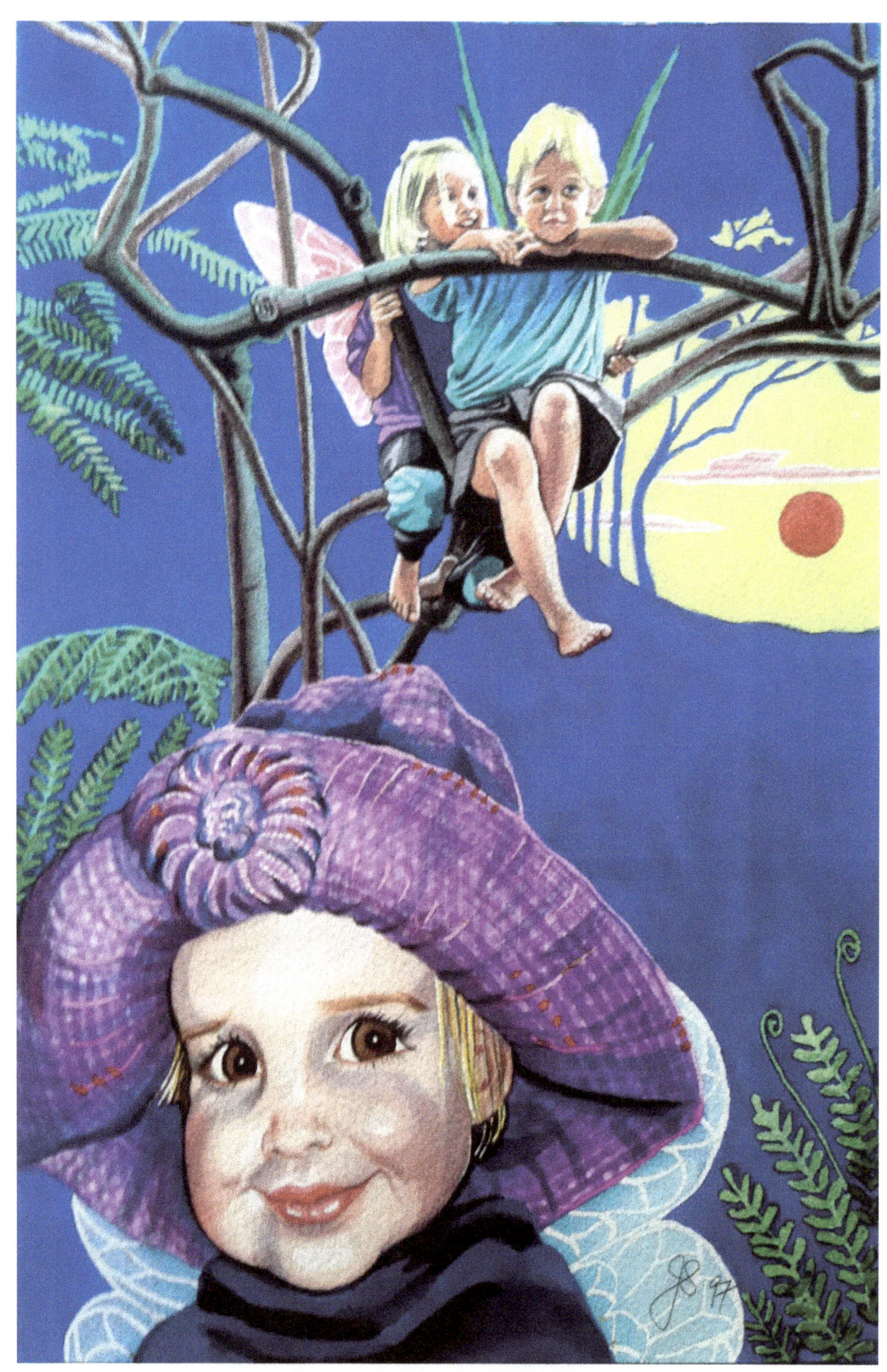

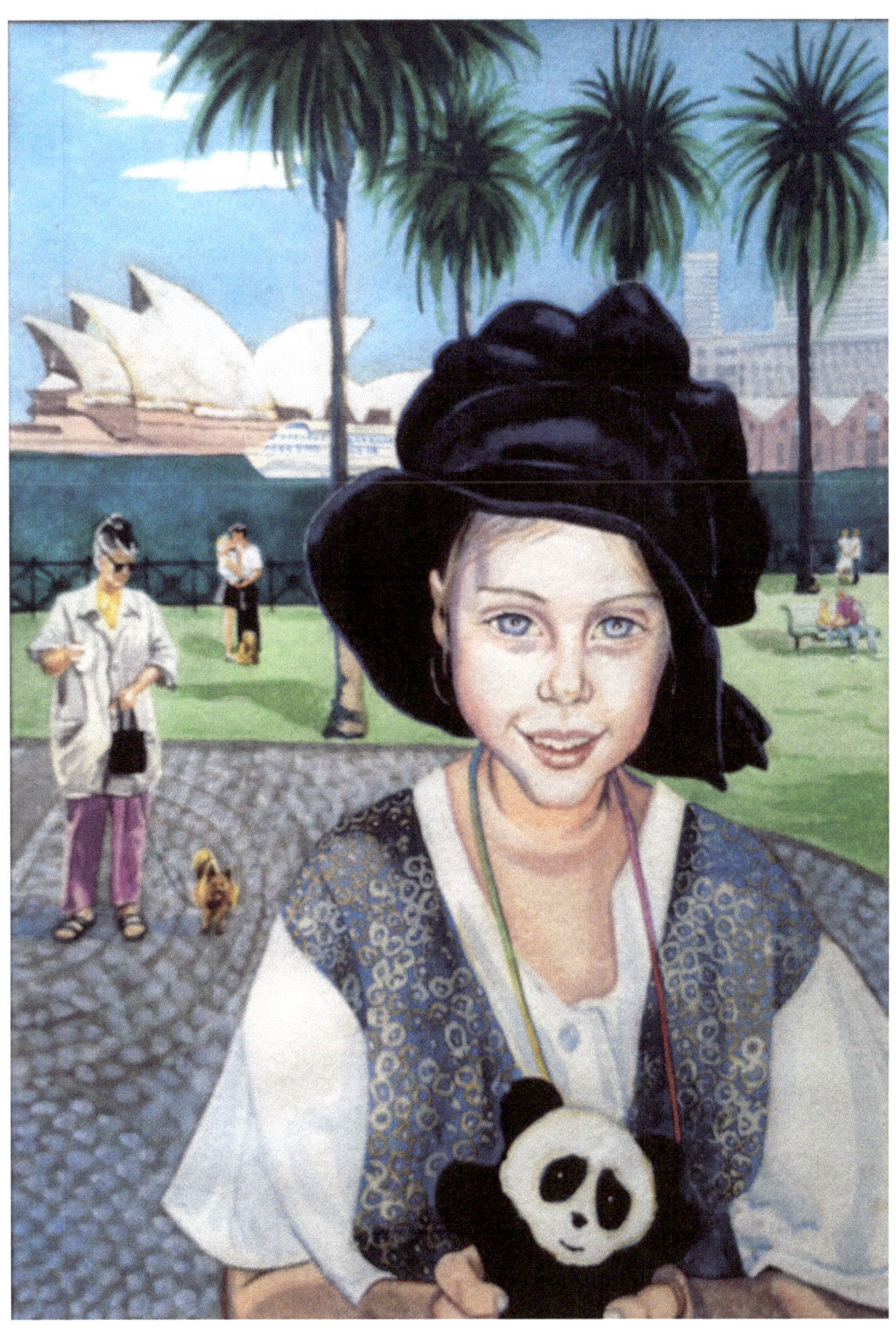

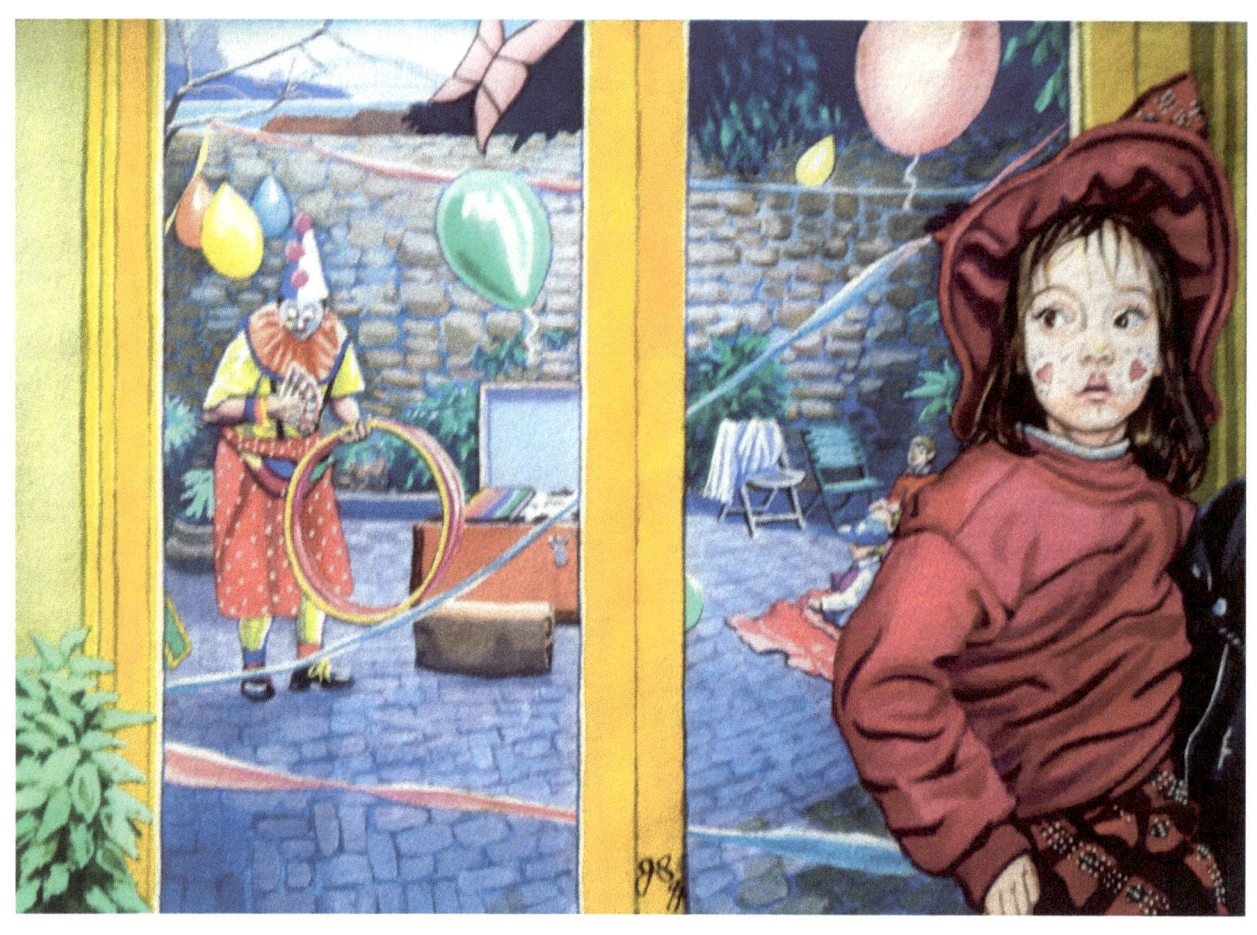

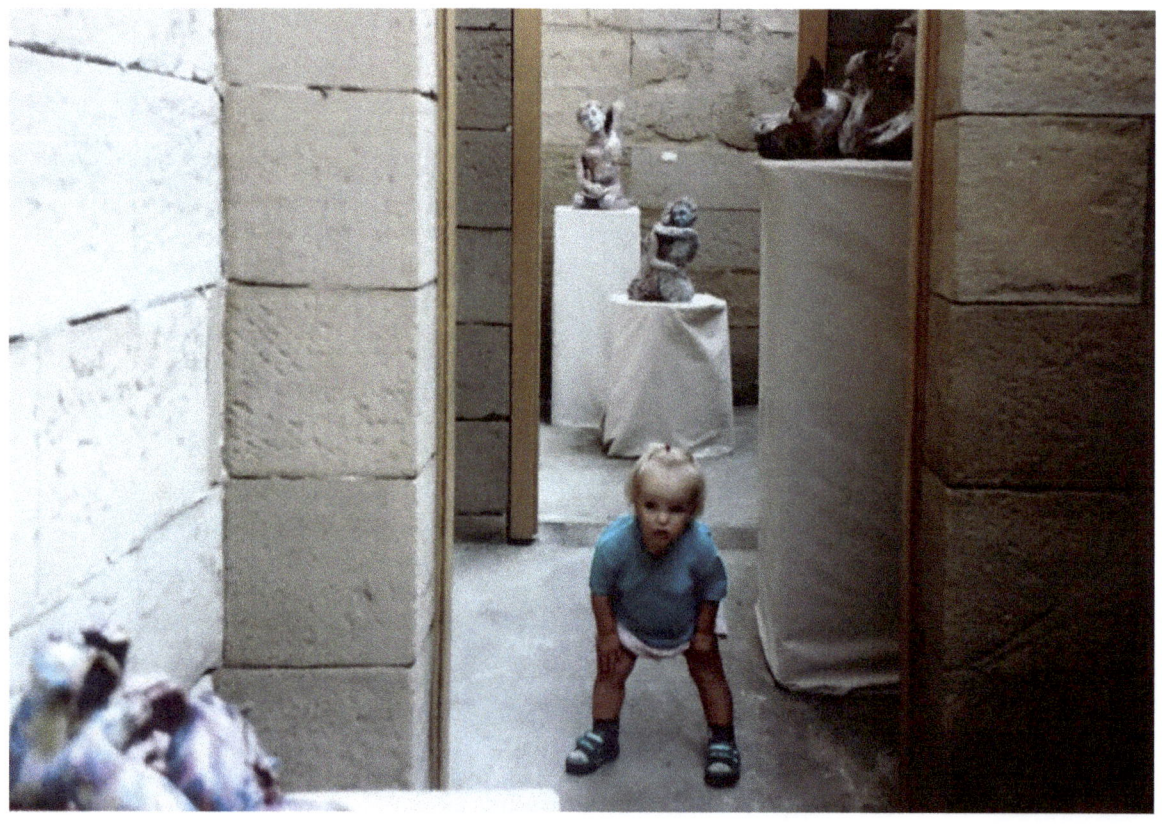

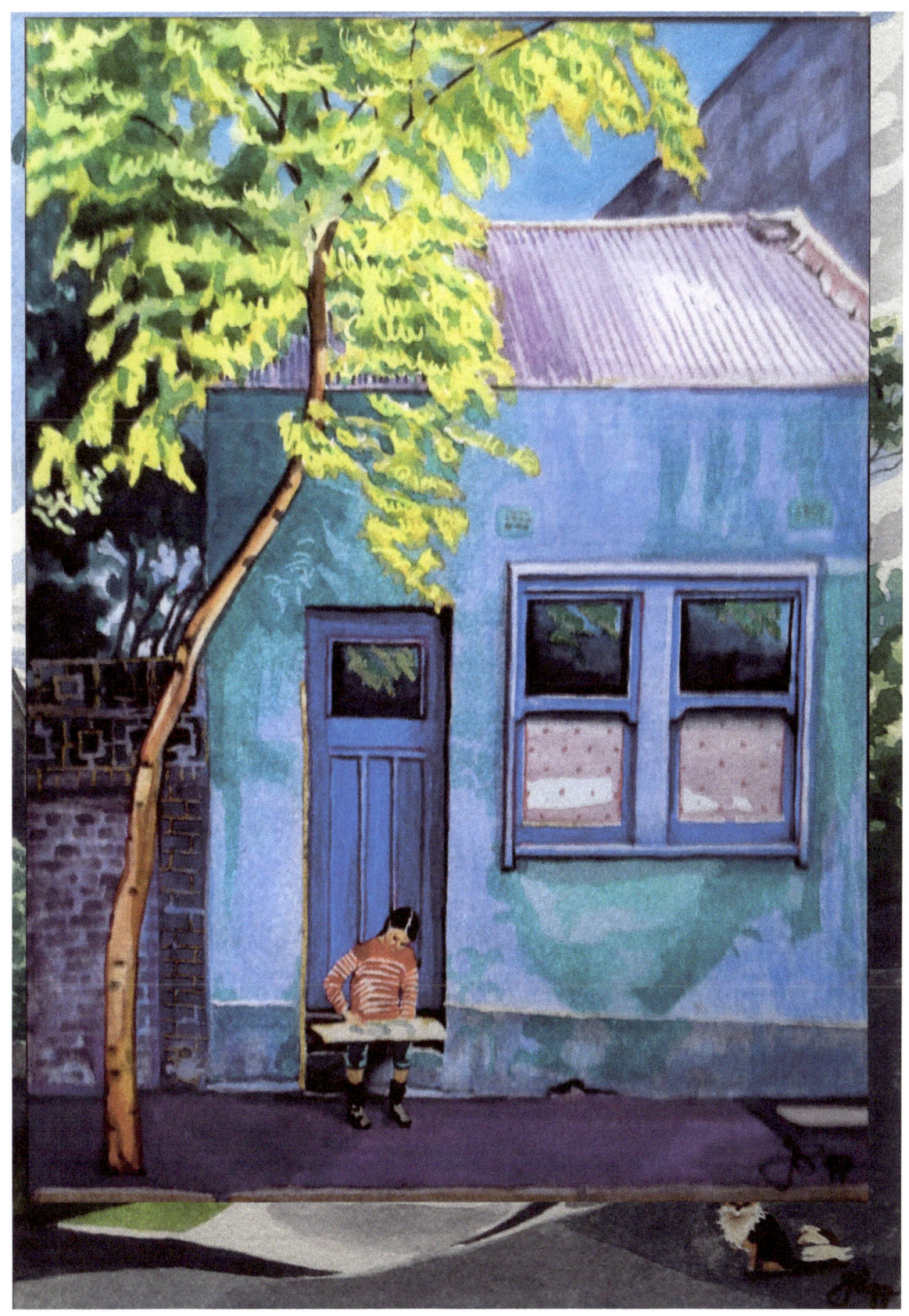

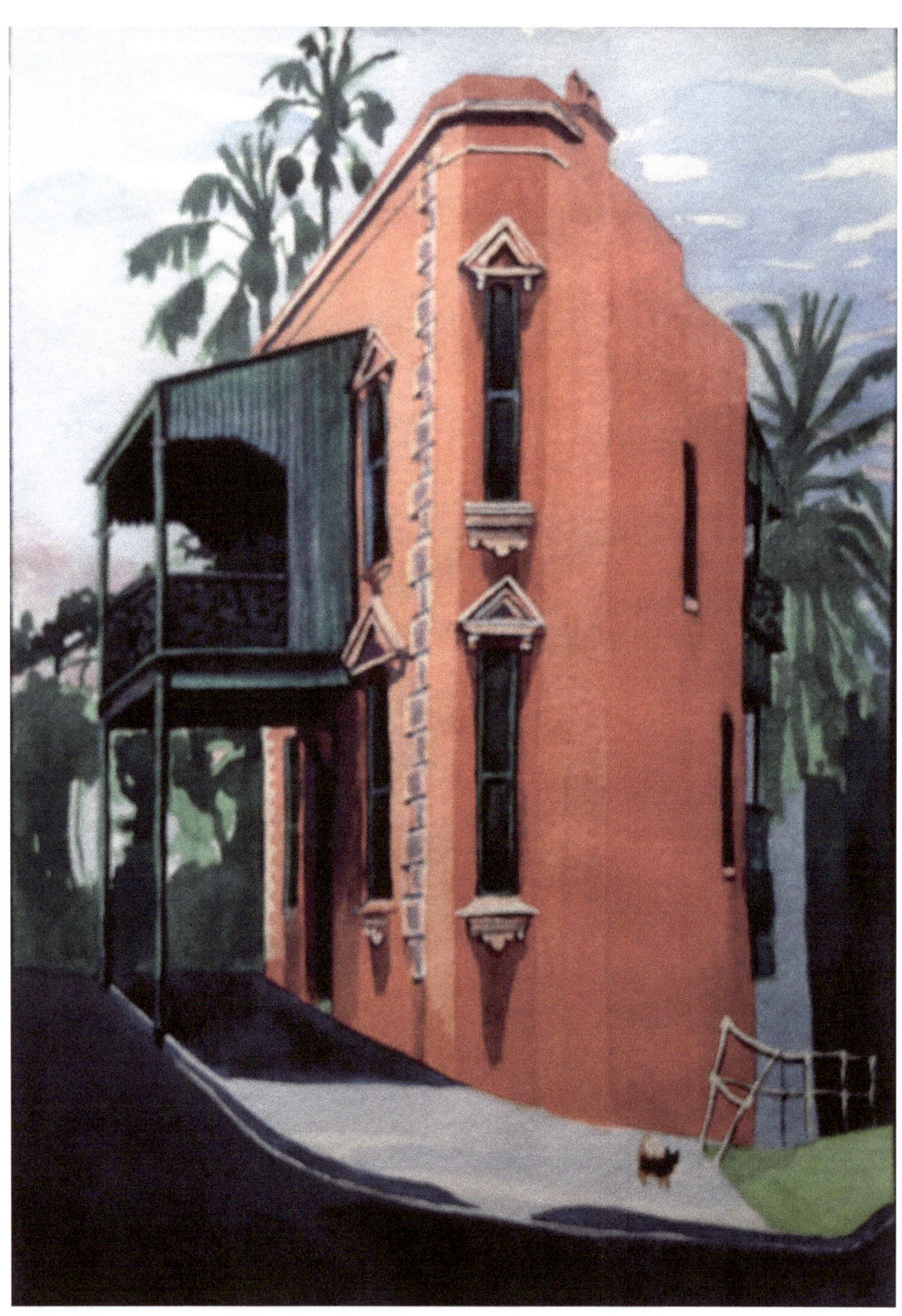

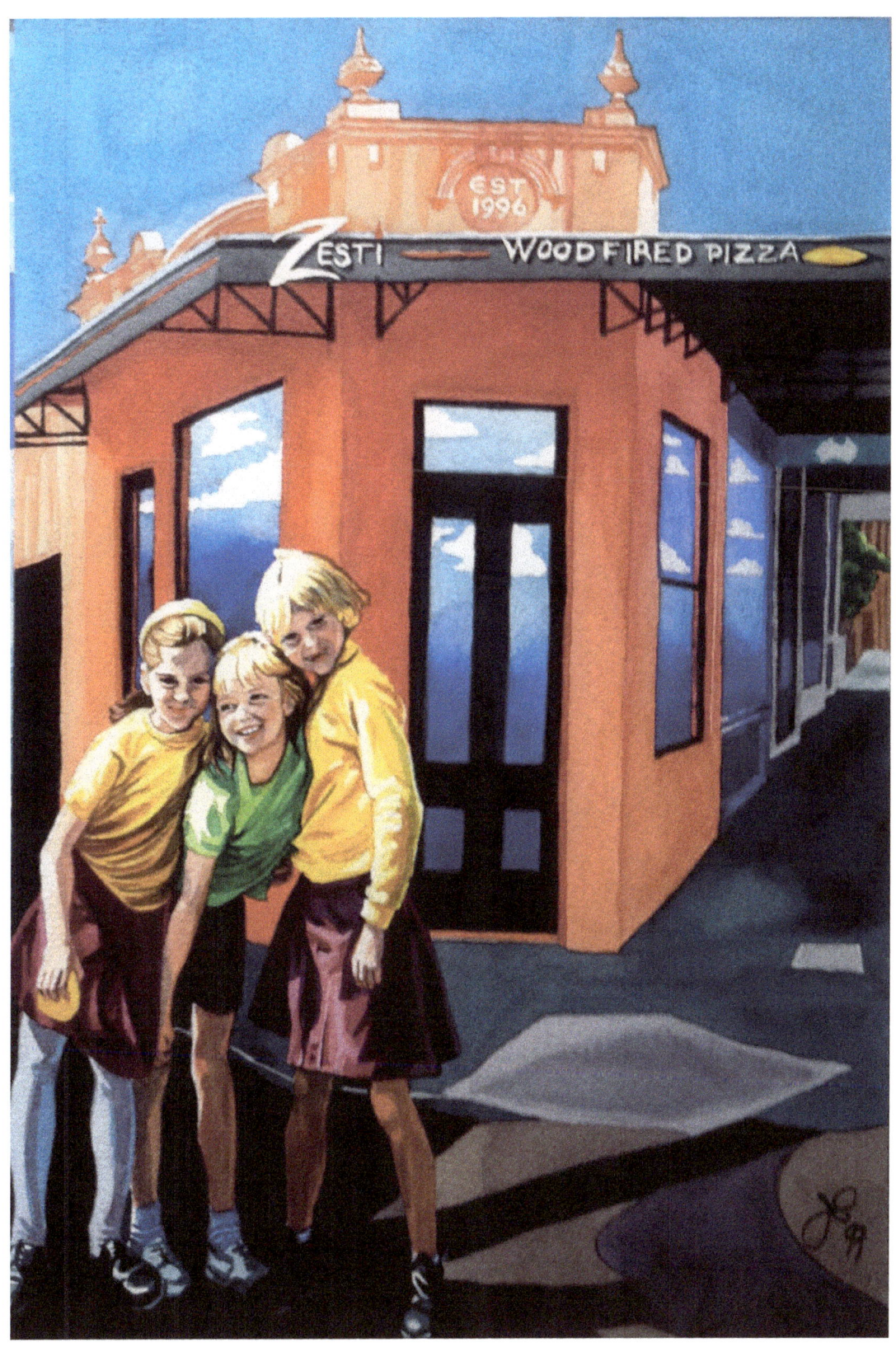

All paintings and photographs by Janet Scott - pp.40 - 51
© Jessica Douglas / Miranda Douglas / Akea Scott
Held in private archival collection

Janet continued her work in her own gallery and below is a list of some works that were catalogued in
LEAP INTO SPRING WITH A LAUGH EXHIBITION at STUDIO FACADE which opened on 26 September, 1982 :

17.	Jane le Rossignol - Rosella	$210.00
19.	Janet Scott - Sid Still lives in Grove Street	$1,500.00
22.	Stephen Dunstan - It Helps If you - Turn Your Rocket Engine On Outside	$145.00
23.	briann - "Bondi Blues" with love at Blakeville"	$80.00

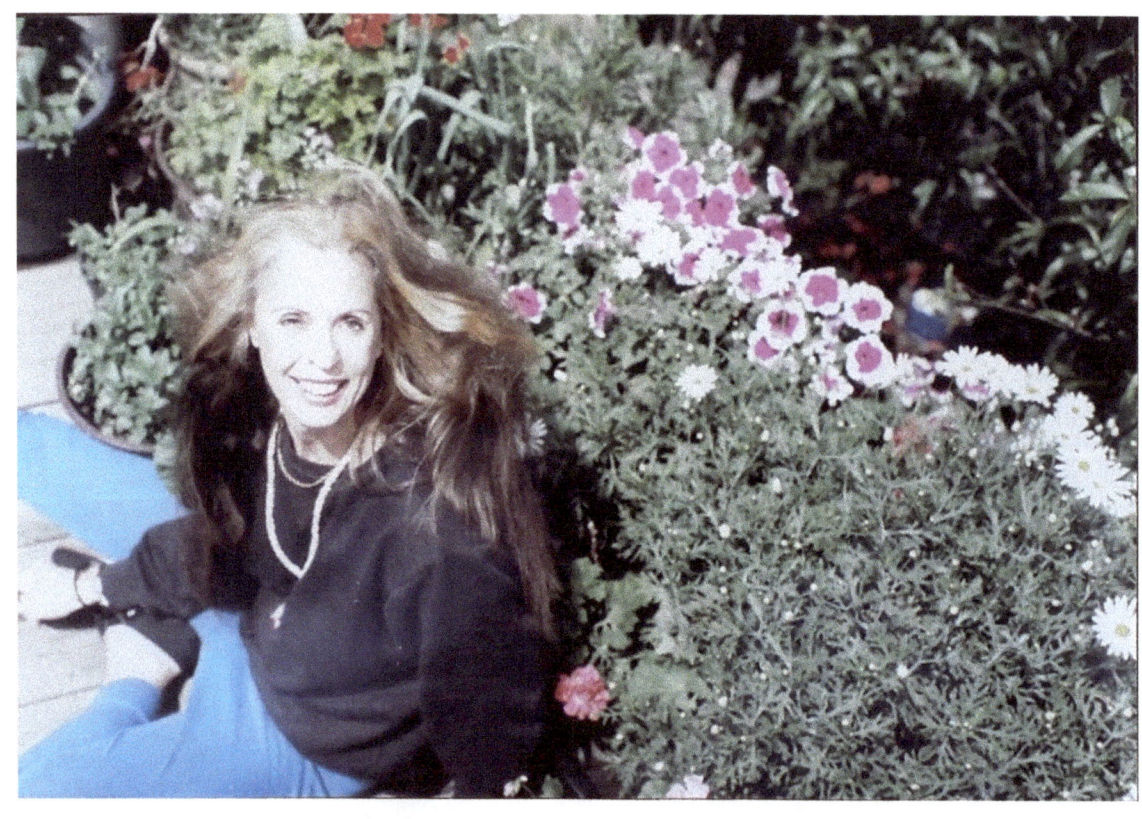

"STUDIO FACADE ROOF GARDEN" (1982)
Photographer : Janet Scott

I think it was about this time, following her return from Canada, that Janet opened a stall at the Balmain Markets ...Sydney's 3rd oldest market established in 1977 at the St. Andrews Congregational Church which was built in 1853 on Cnr. Darling Street and Curtis Road, Balmain.

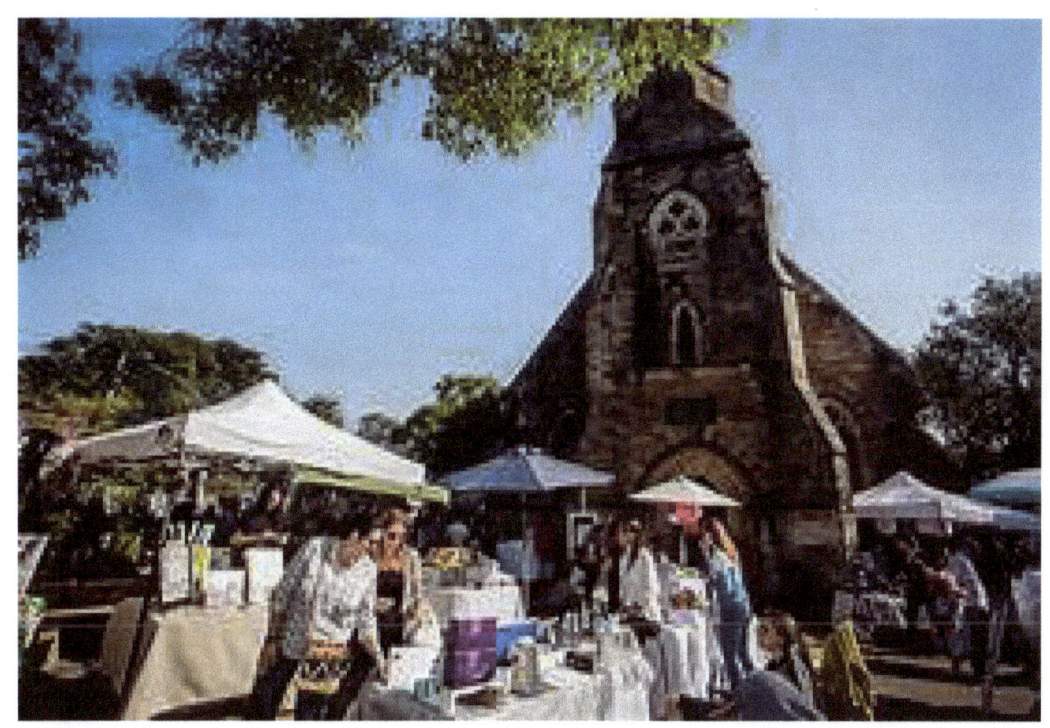

Balmain market
www.sydneycom

It was also around this time that Janet moved into her pottery stage acquiring a kiln and setting it up in her tiny, tiny back garden and producing some amazing pieces. I acquired 2 x small pottery bowls from the very first batch that Janet made plus 2 x large glazed "GUM TREE" plates - one for myself and the other for Beverley Ward (aka Beverley Thompson). I do know that Kevin always regretted not being able to buy one of Janet's delightfully fey teapots to add to our "teapot" collection but as I recall they were not for sale and remained in Janet's own pottery collection.

STUDIO FACADE
at
Balmain Markets Saturday
Original Works
Jewellery & Watercolours

STUDIO FACADE
THE APHOTO-RILISM SHOW
Opening – APRIL FOOLS DAY 1983
Close   – April 30th

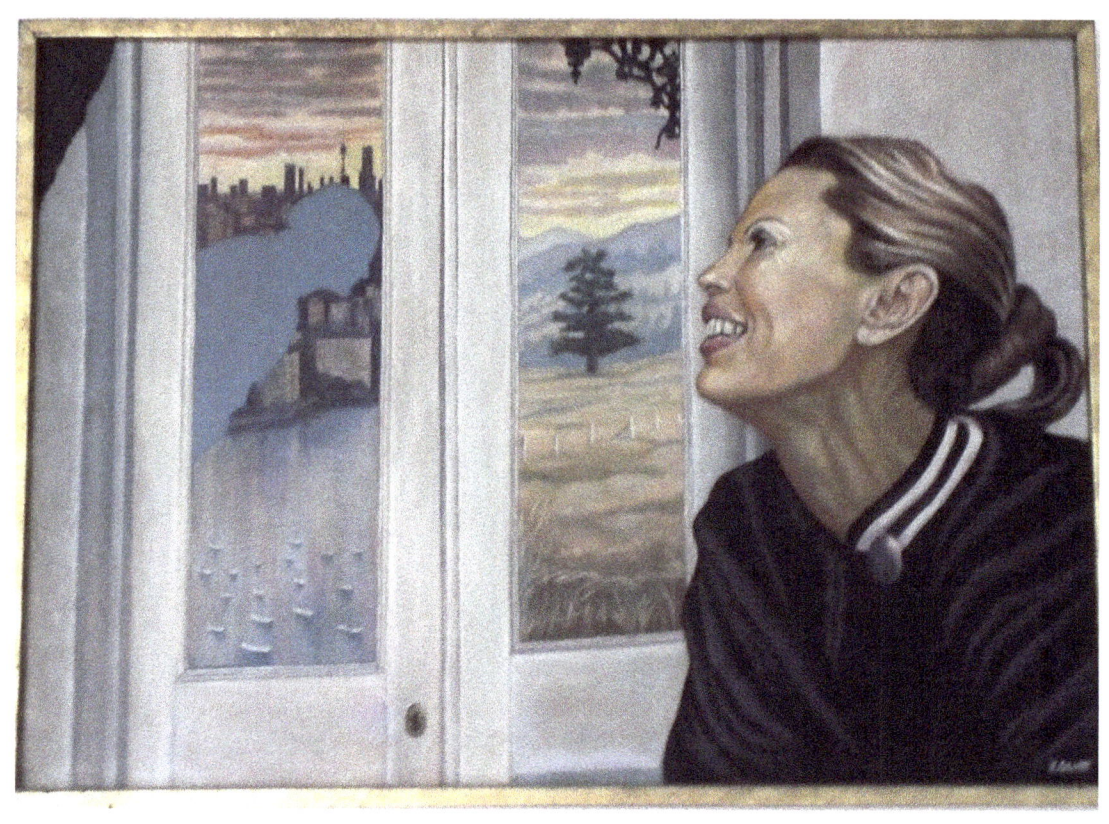

No. 3 – EMOH WEN RUO (1983)
Artist : Janet Scott
Method : Oil & Egg tempera
Price : $550.00

On 13 January, 1983 ANTARES GALLERY Group Exhibition took place at The School of Arts, 275c Pitt Street, Sydney and among Janet's contributions was the photo realist portrait based on the photograph "ADMIRING THE VIEW" (1980) taken by Janet on the balcony of "Blakeville".

This painting is the first time that Janet had used the egg tempera method. Art Web advises that for centuries egg tempera was the preferred medium for panel paintings and that many of the masterpieces from the medieval and renaissance were executed in egg tempera.

It appears it was used in the ancient world on such famous pieces as the life-like Fayum mummy portraits produced in Egypt around the 1st century BC to the 3rd century AD.. Egg tempera is considered to be more durable than oil, possessing a luminosity similar to watercolour yet offering to the artist many advantages, advantages that Janet was willing to embrace in order to work in this ancient medium.

You are cordially invited to
MYTH AND BEASTS
an exhibition of garden sculpture
by Janet Scott
Paintings by Michael Joyce
Screen Prints by Clemency Browne
at
The Watch House
179 Darling Street, Balmain
Opening 6. November, 1990

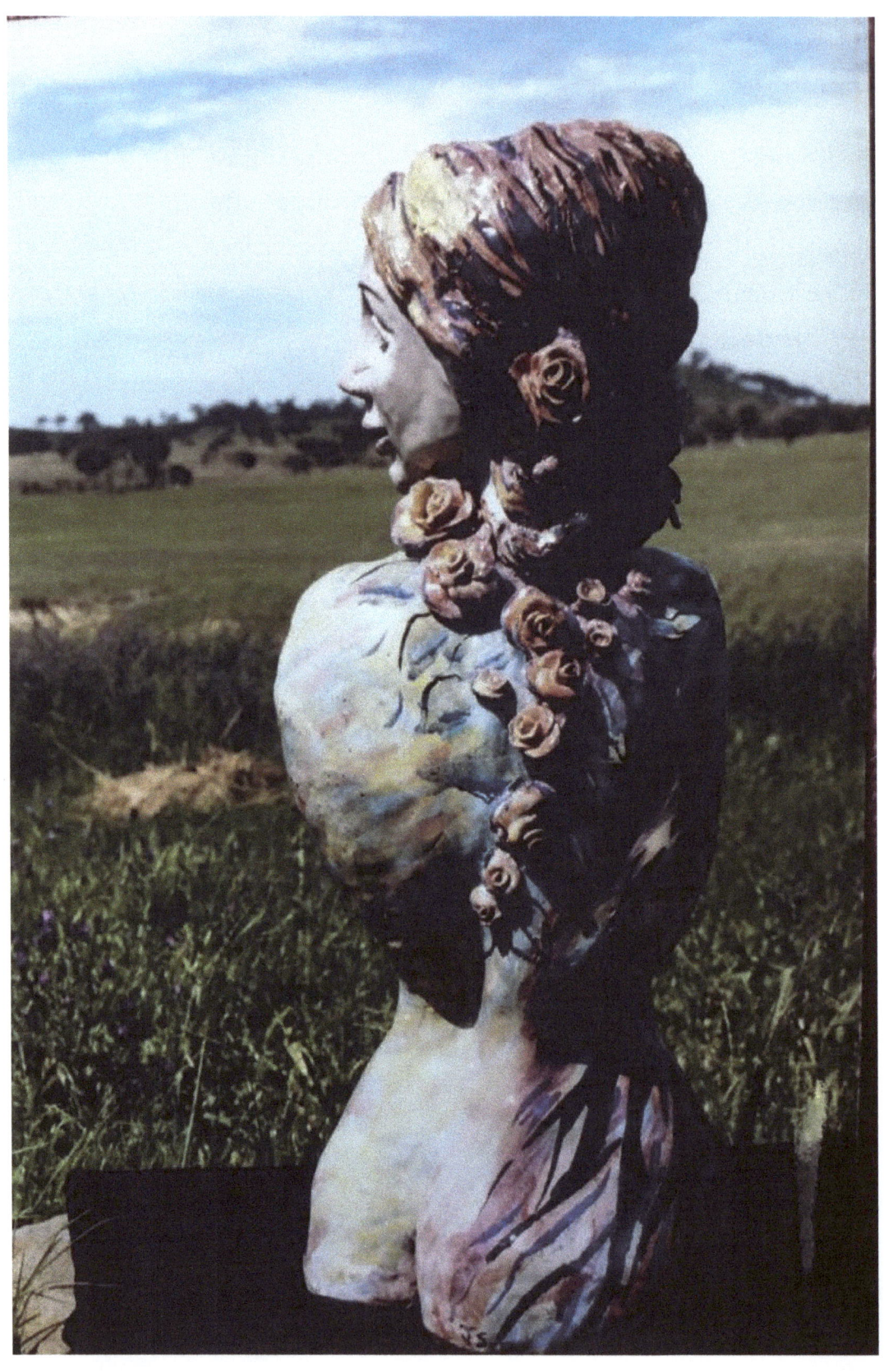

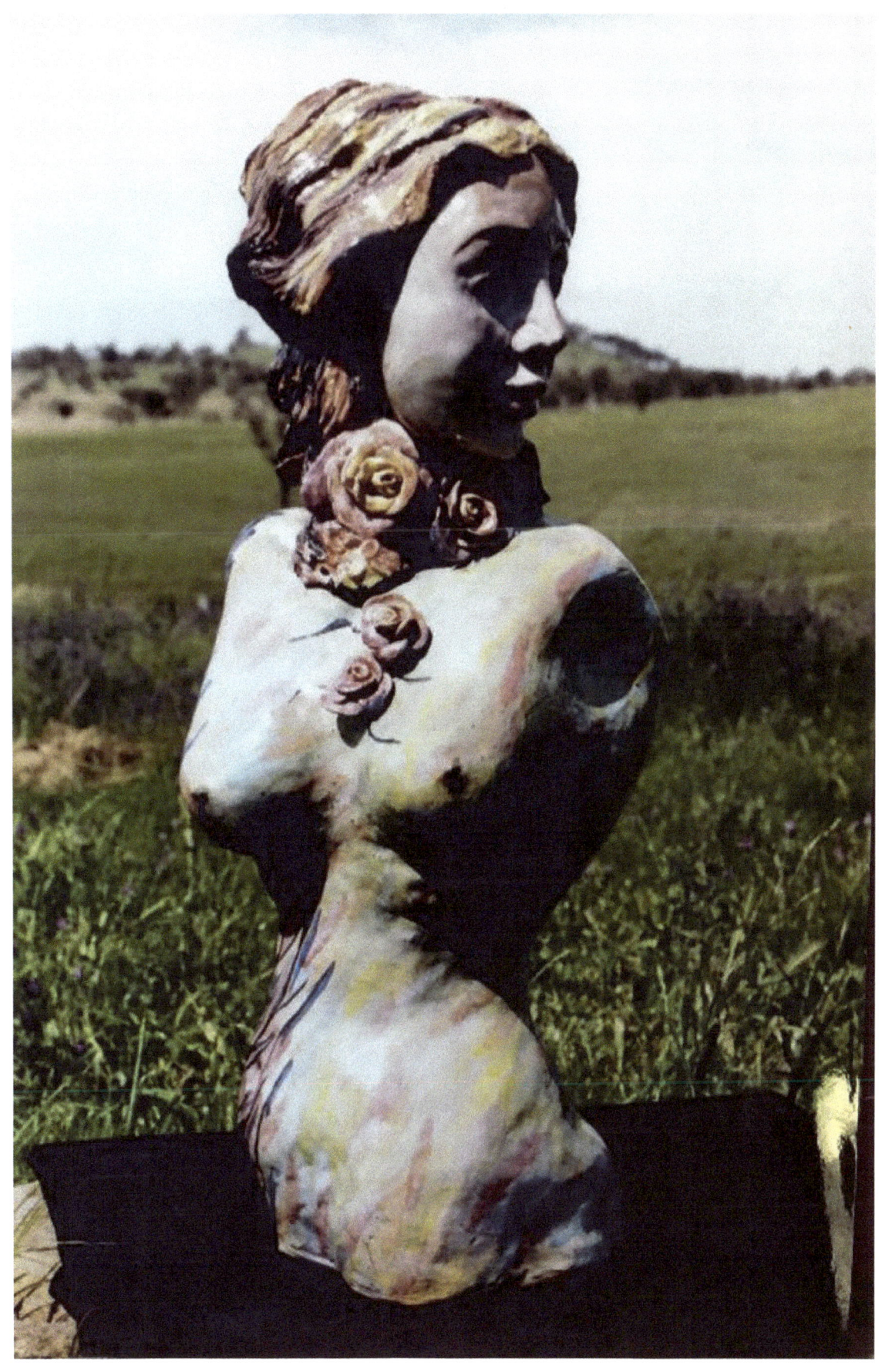

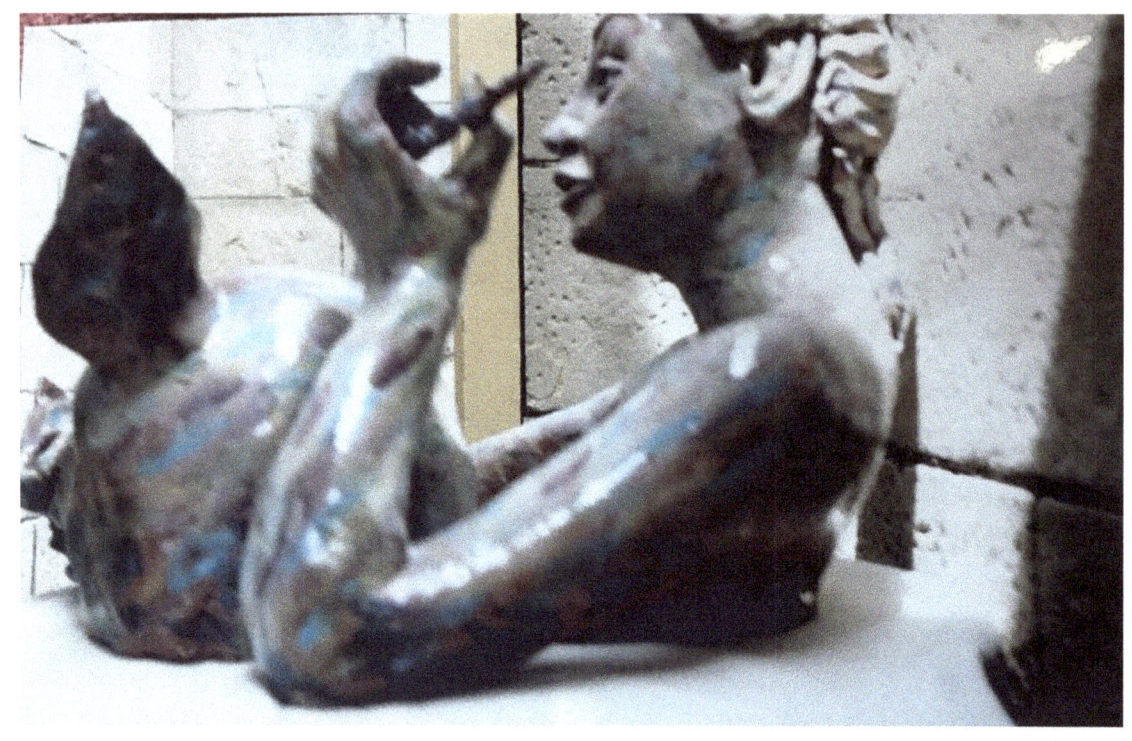

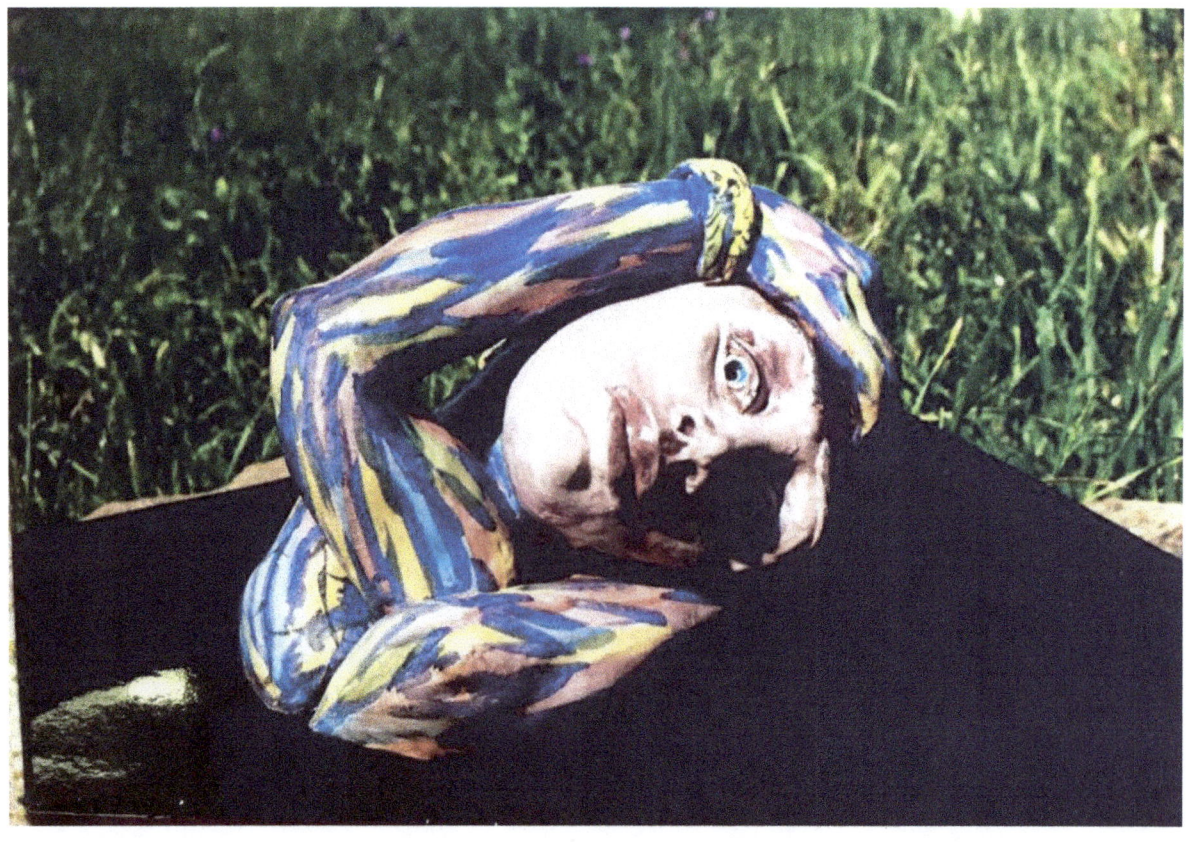

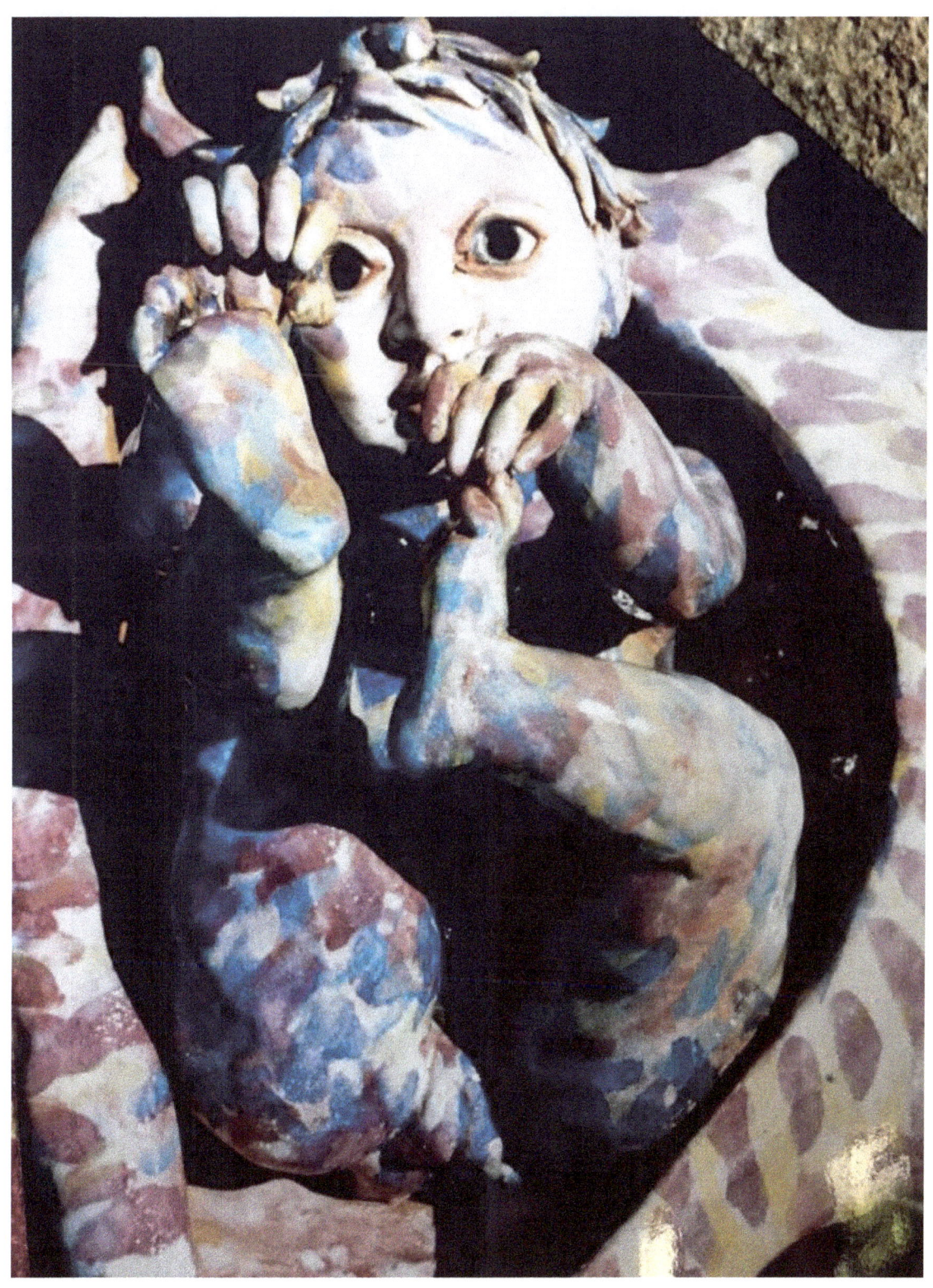

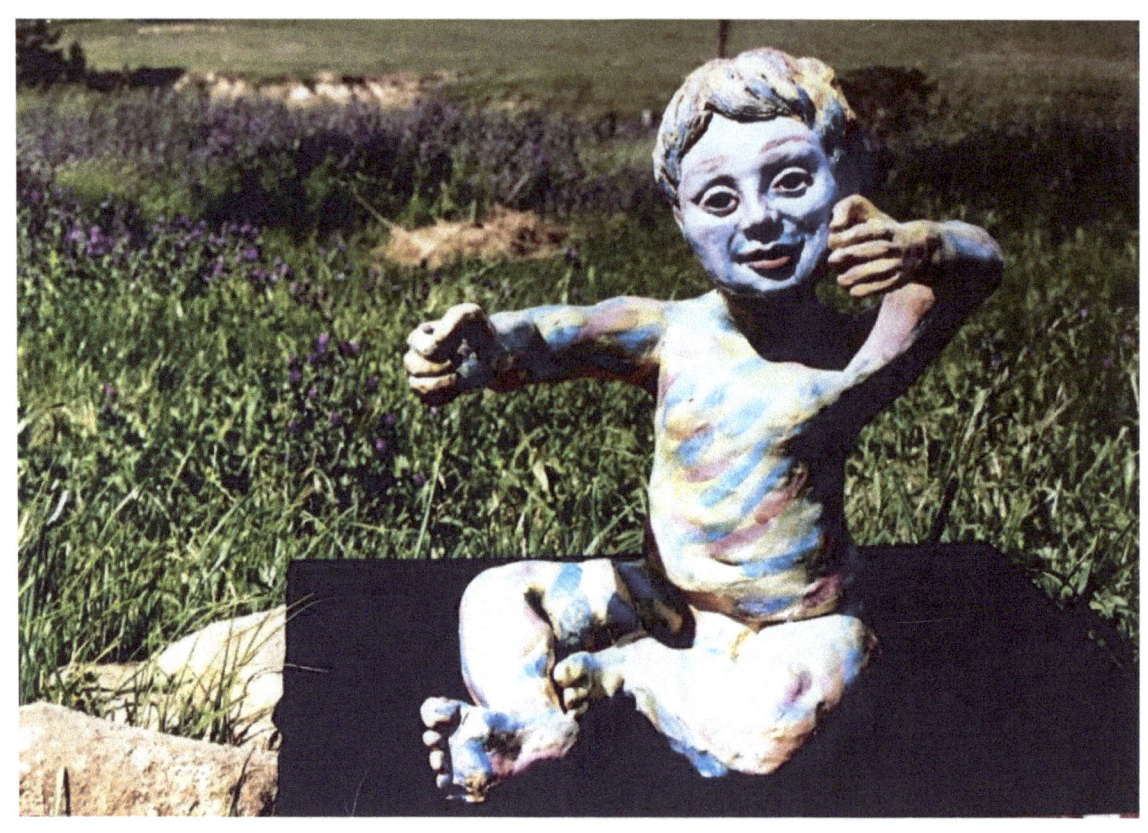

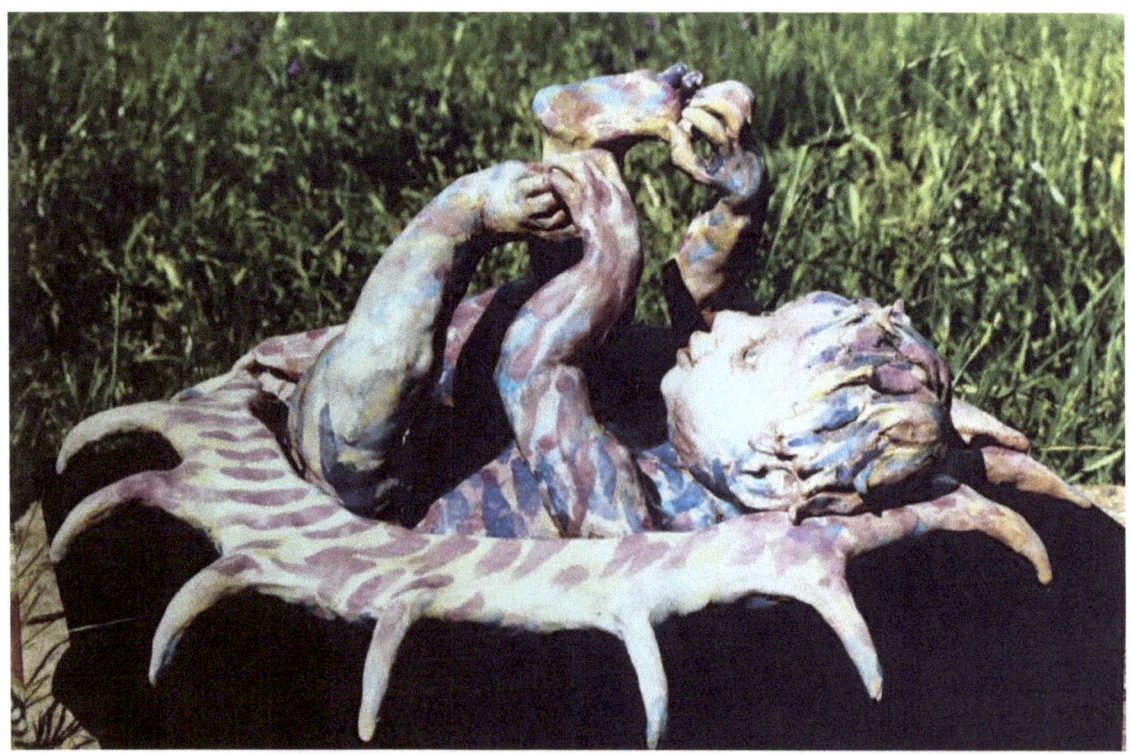

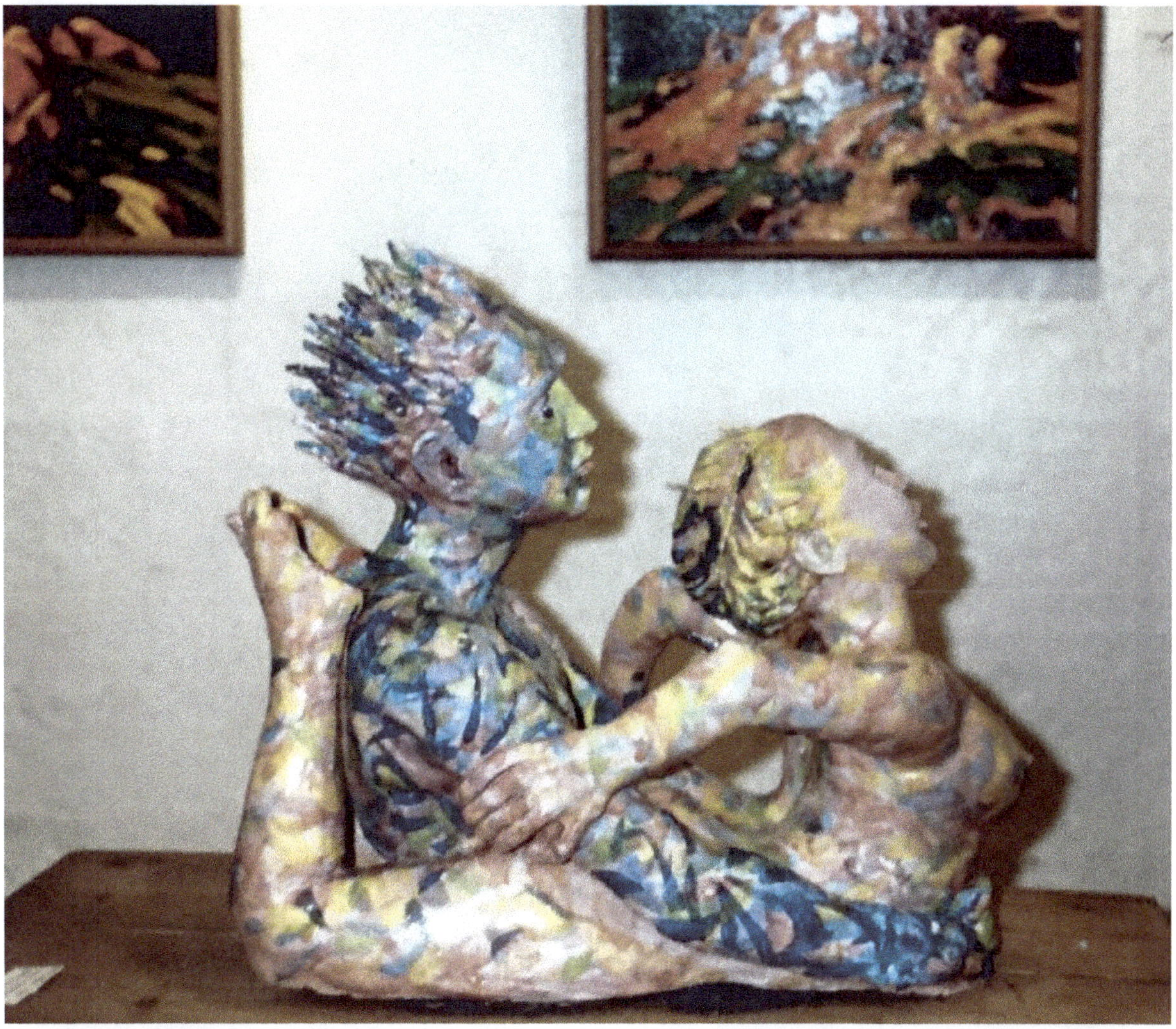

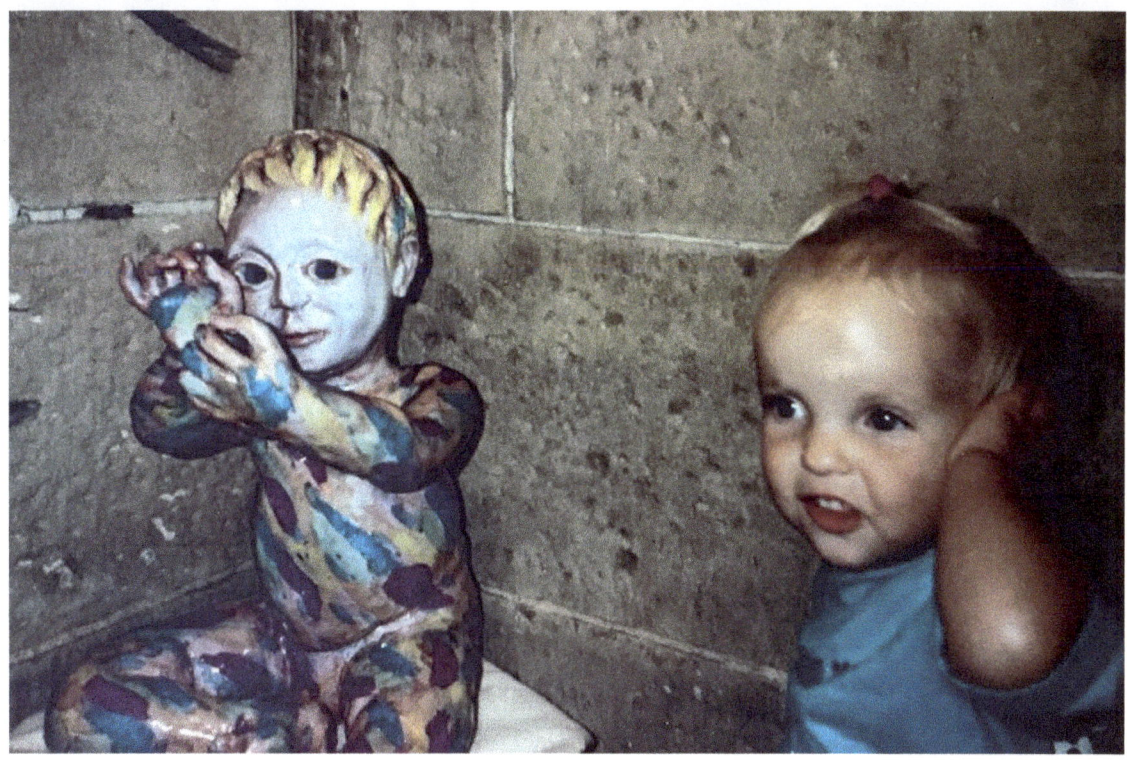

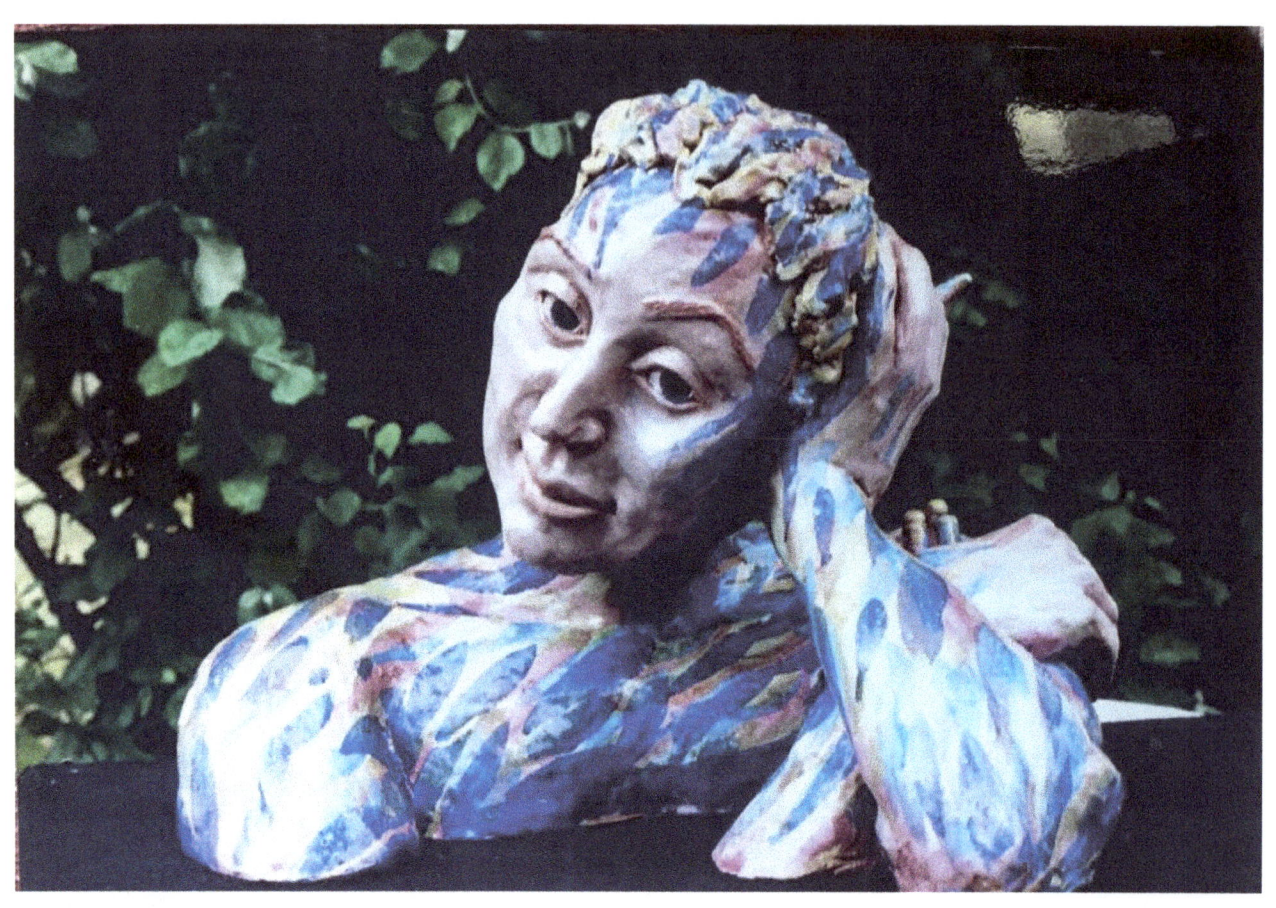

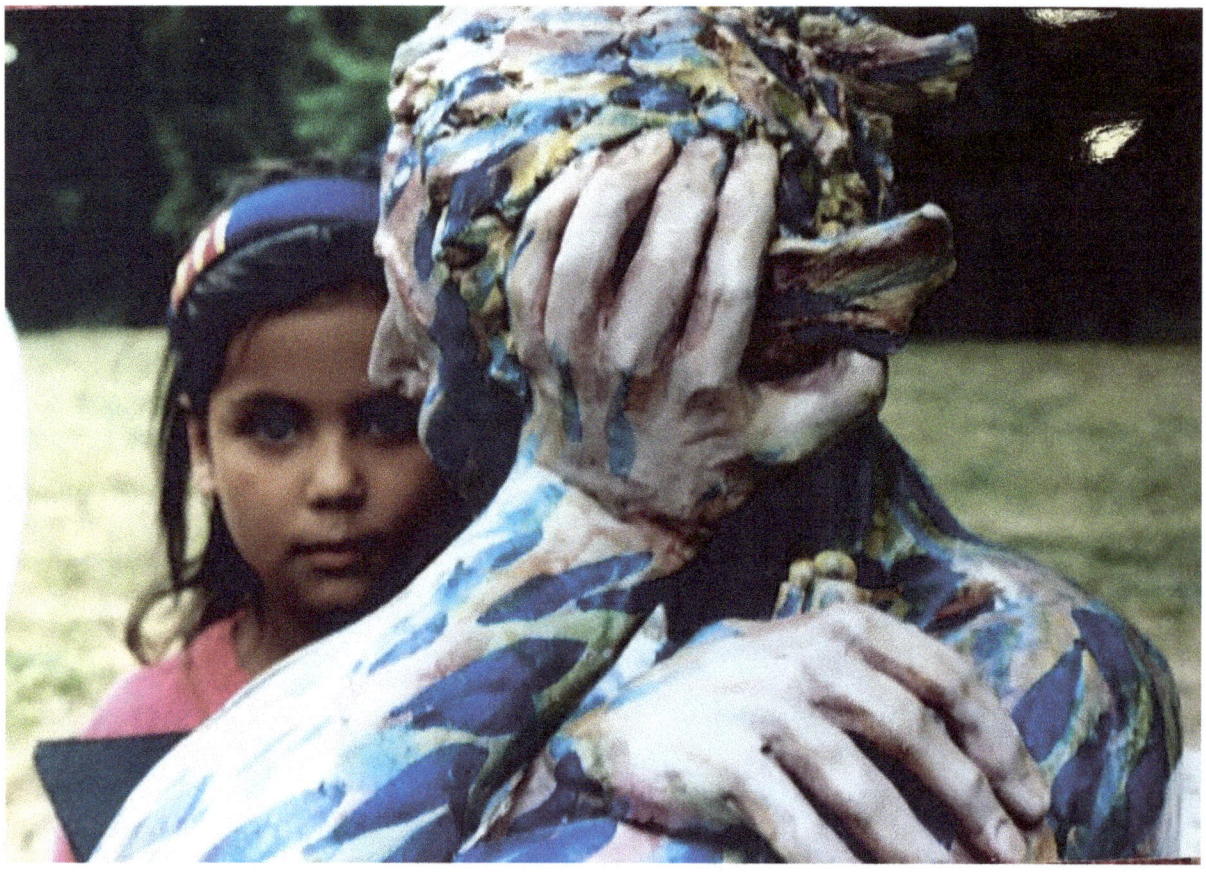

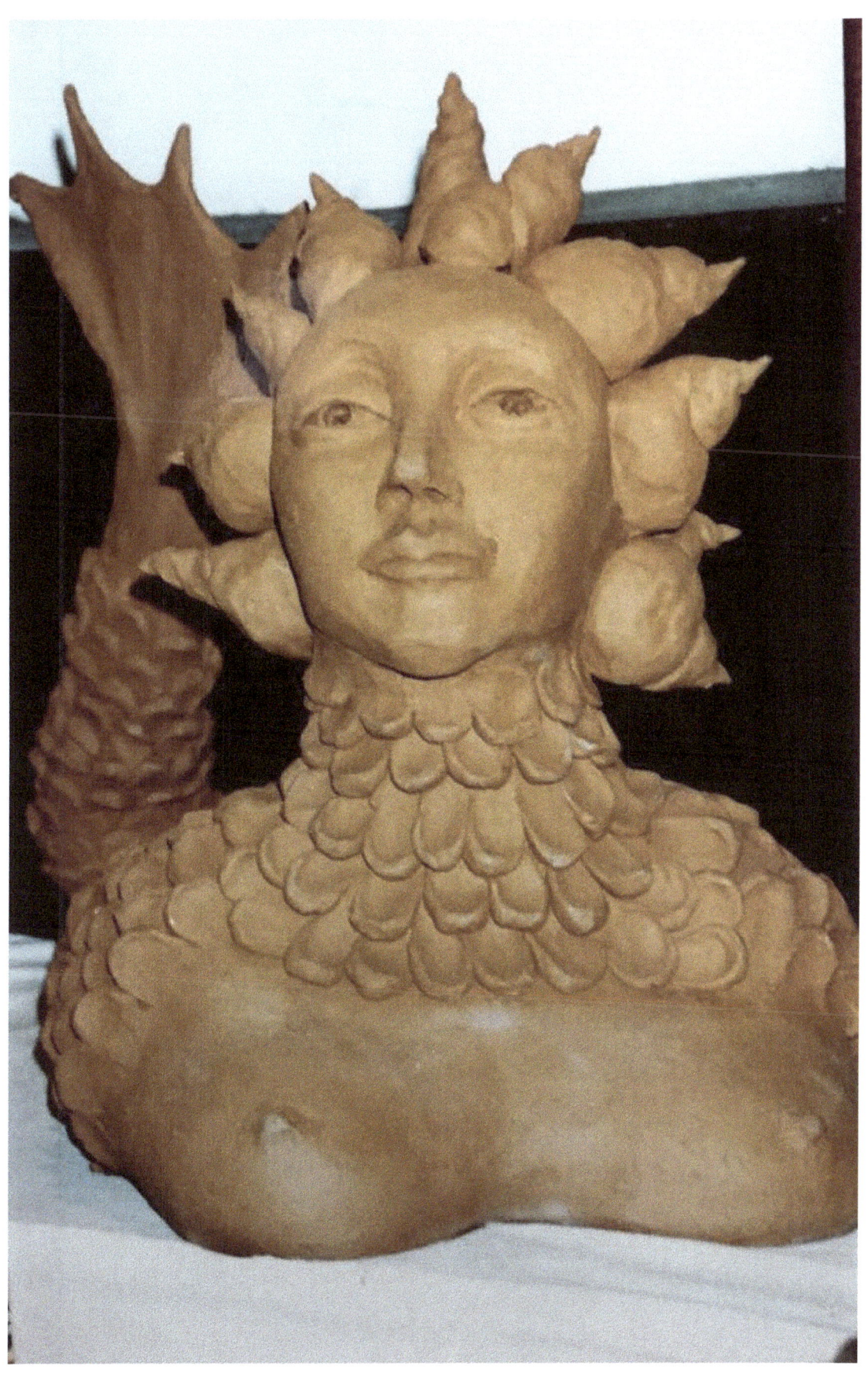

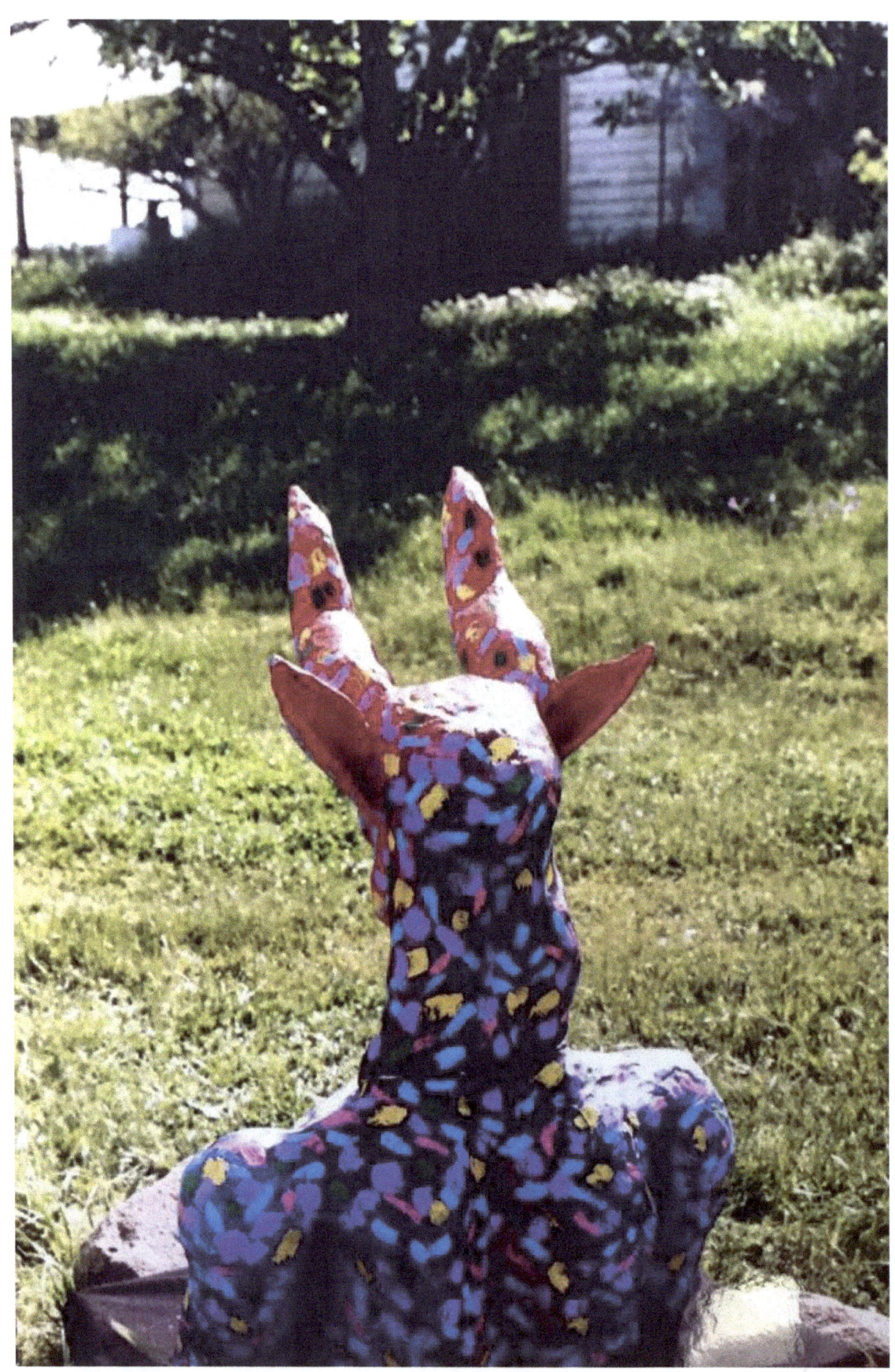

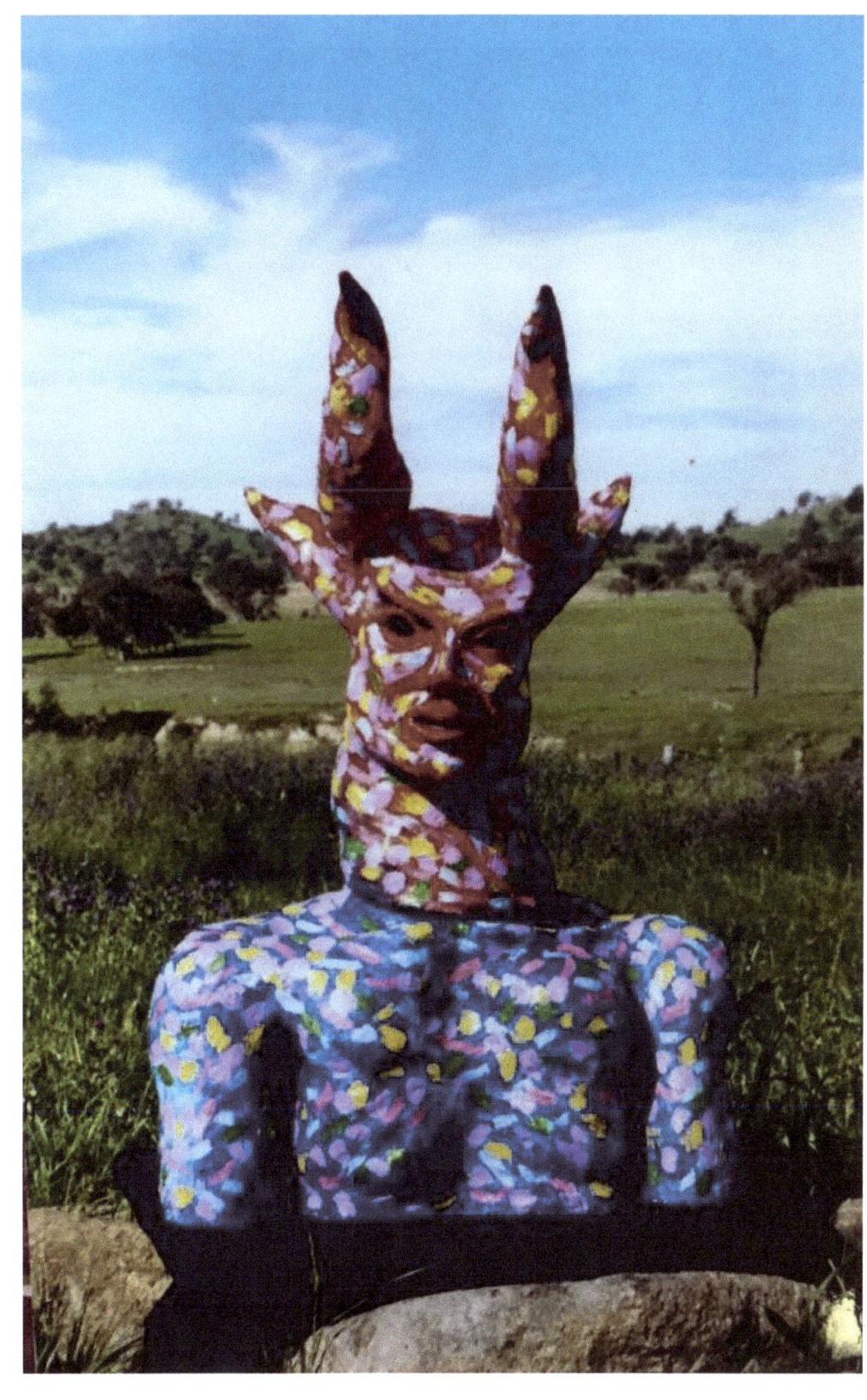

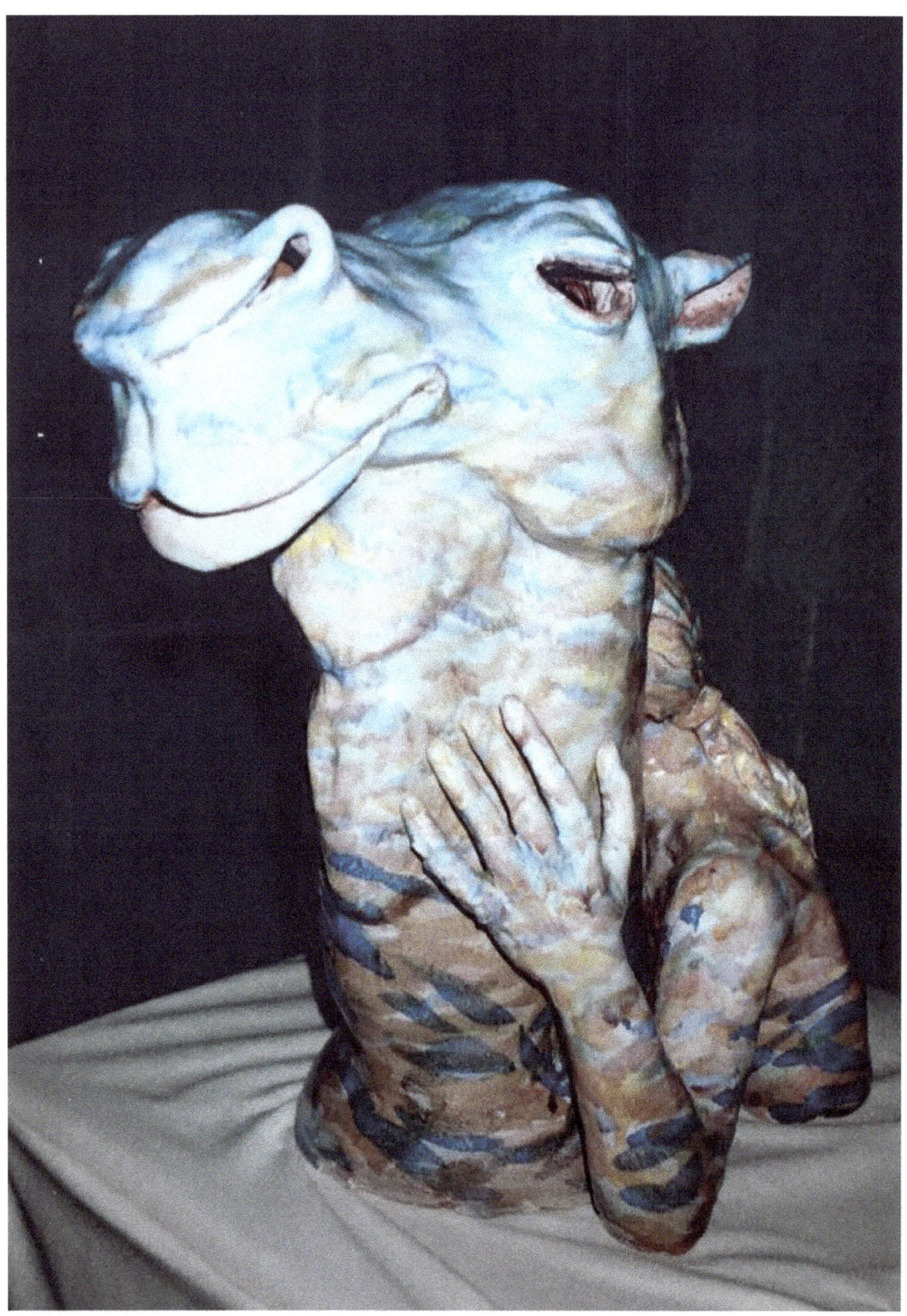

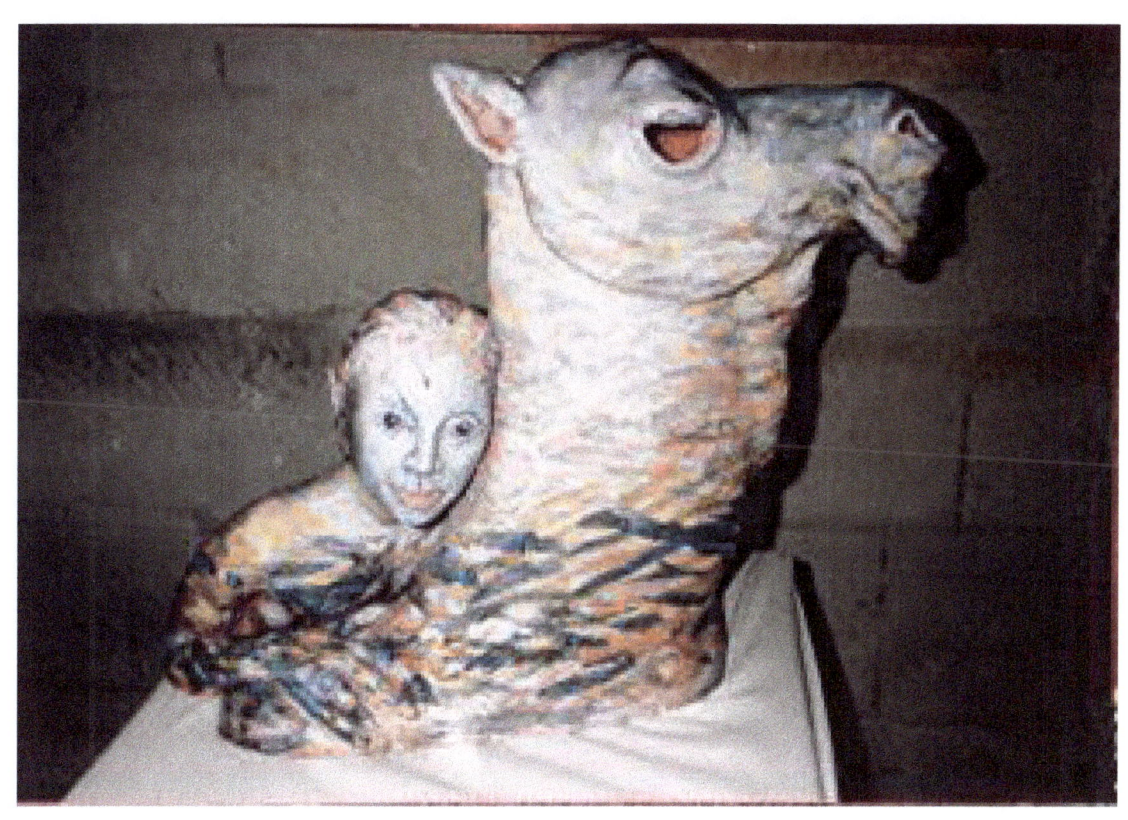

All sculptures and photographs by Janet Scott - pp.55 - 66
© Jessica Douglas / Miranda Douglas / Akea Scott
Held in private archival collection

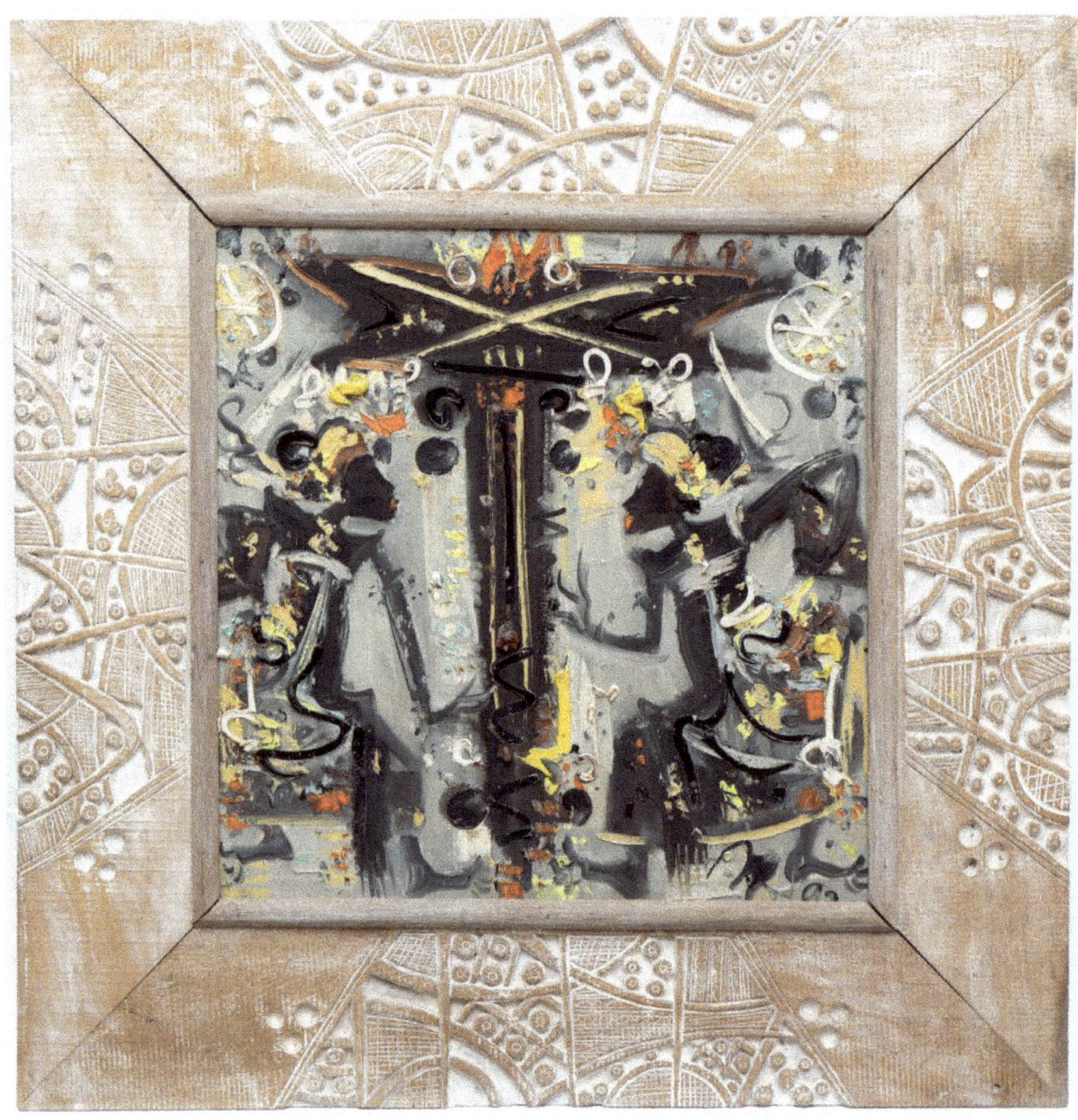

One of the international artists that STUDIO FACADE hosted in 1984 was Nyoman Gunarsa (1944 - 2017) whose "signature style was an adaptation from western art in which the individual's innovative ideas, emotions and energy are omnipotent.

STUDIO FACADE PRESENTS
OFFERINGS
Sesaji & Aringgit
Paintings by
Nyoman Gunarsa
Opening May 23, 1984

Raised in the village of Kamasan which during the 16 - 20th century was the epicentre of Balinese Classical culture, Gunarsa was renowned for his dedication to the art of his forefathers. In the 1980s his fresh approach to depicting the characters of the Wayang Kulit shadow puppet theatre broke new aesthetic grounds in Balinese art."

Janet met Nyoman and his wife on her several visits to Bali and an exhibition of his work was arranged in concert with his exhibition at the Solandor Art Gallery, Yarralumla, Canberra.

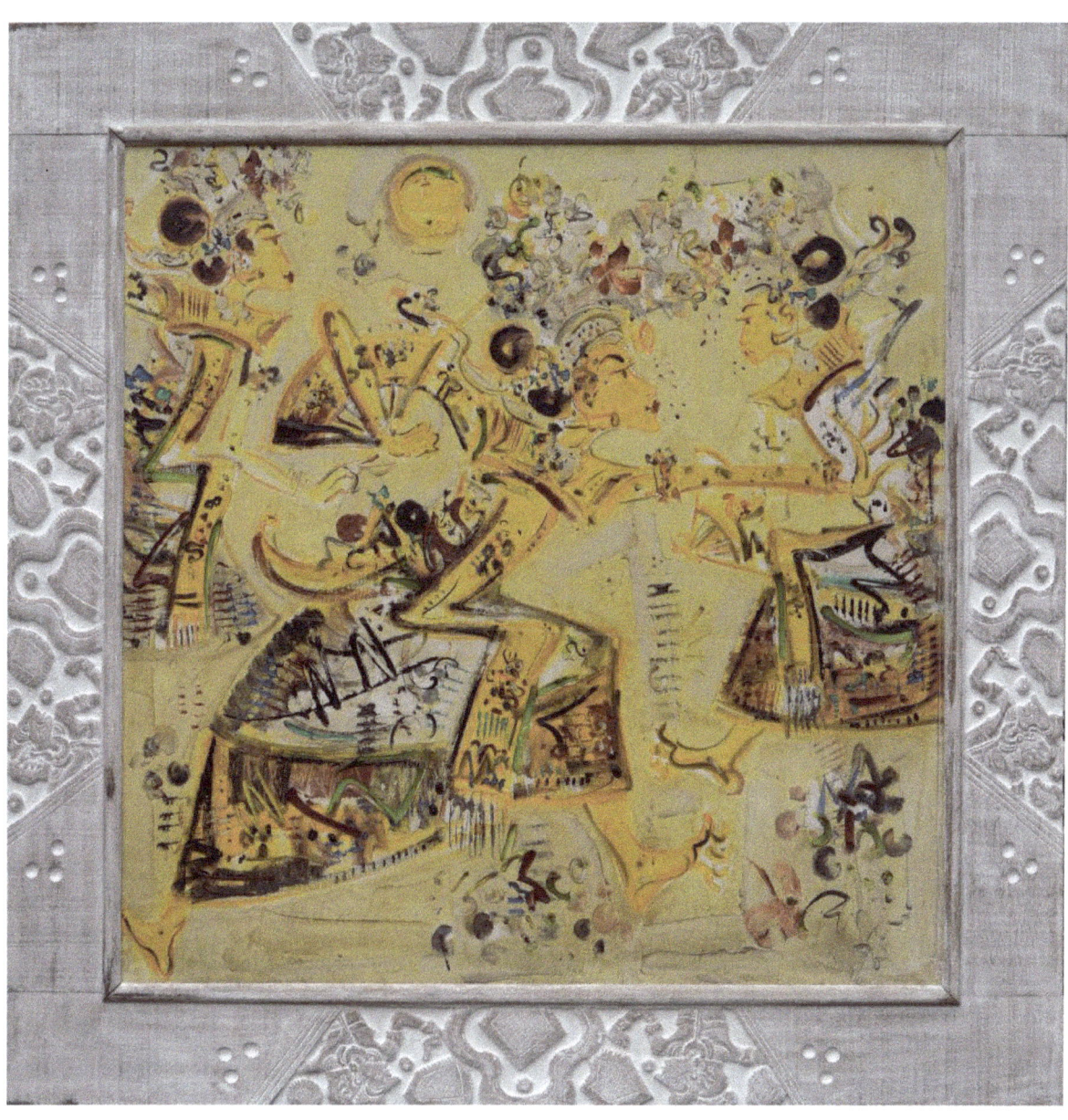

While Nyoman was in Australia Janet organised for STUDIO FACADE to co-produce, with Teapot Cottage Industries, a 30 minute documentary of his visit to Birchgrove.

NYOMAN GUNARSA - ARTIST (1984)

Producer	Janet Scott
Director	briann
Camera	Nixon Binney
Sound	Kevin Kearney
Artist	Nyoman Gunarsa
Locations :	1. Park, opp. 104 Foucart St., Rozelle
	2. Kate Holland, Louisa Rd., Birchgrove
	3. STUDIO FACADE Bay & Grove Sts., Birchgrove

Synopsis :

Nyoman Gunarsa discussed his work / his painting exhibition @ STUDIO FACADE / as well as performing his traditional dance on the harbour front in Louisa Rd. Birchgrove. This documentary screened at Nyoman Gunarsa's Museum Seni Lukis Klasik, Jalaan Pertigaan Banda No. 1, Takmung, Banjarangkan following its opening in 1990

Unfortunately Janet's health was not 100% and although she still kept working prodigiously keeping the gallery open for her almost monthly exhibitions was proving to be just a step too far. By late 1985 STUDIO FACADE held its final group showing although the gallery itself opened spasmodically for individual artists and remained a showplace for Janet's own work until she left Sydney.

1990   THE CHRONICLES OF ICARUS
Retold, illustrated and published by Janet Scott
Designed by Jennifer Gormley
ISBN 0 646 00831 5

Janet Scott's striking drawings illustrate her allegorical tale of mankinds journey through birth, life and death. Janet has signed this book and it is a limited edition but I don't know how many were printed.

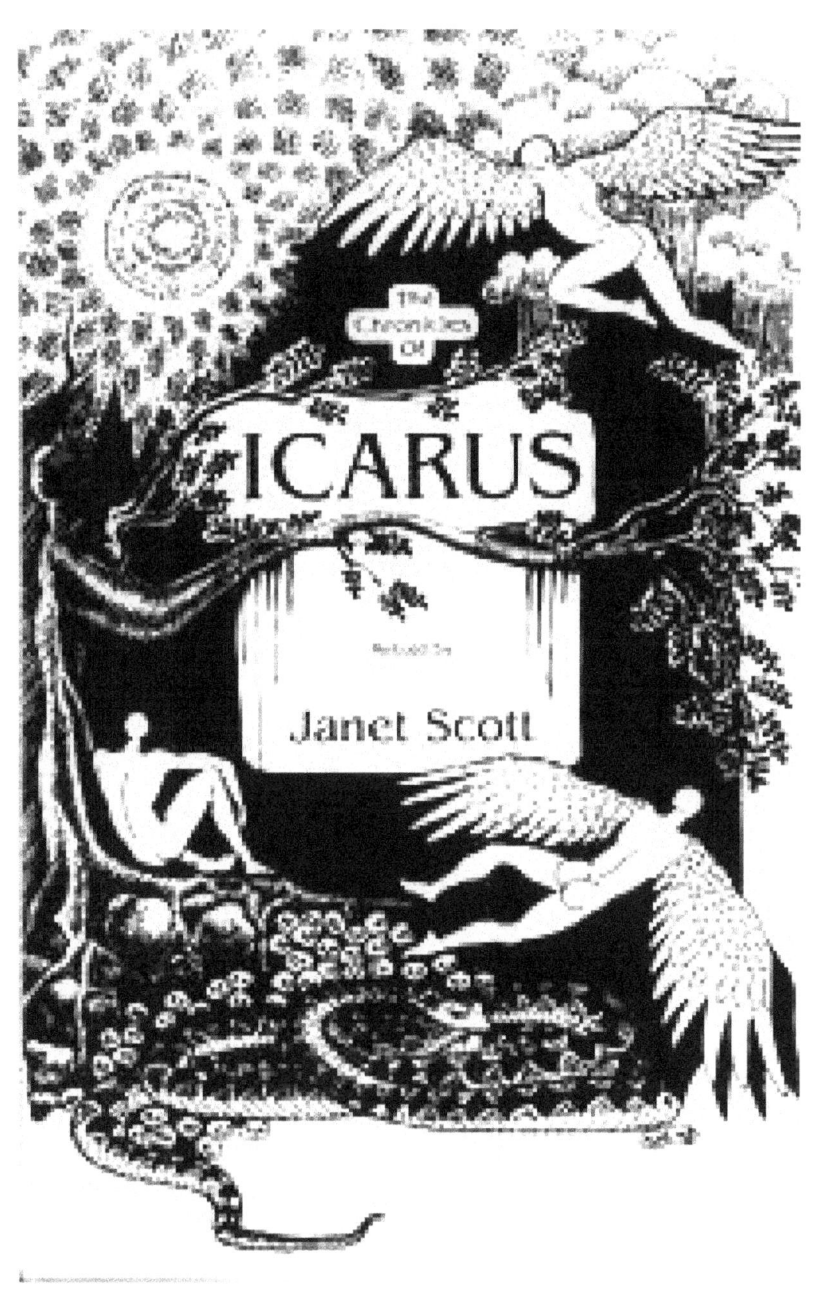

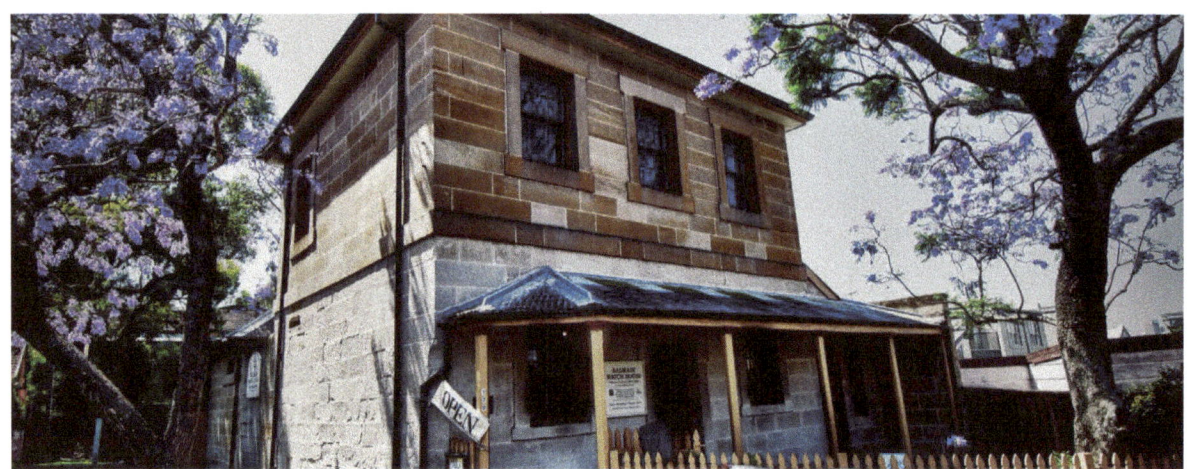

1990   POTS 'N' PRINTS FOR CHRISTMAS
                      Group Exhibition
                      The Balmain Watchhouse,
                      Balmain

An article about this exhibition and Janet's work appeared in the 1990 - April Issue - OPEN ROAD - "JANET SCOTT'S POTS" /

The Edmund Blackett designed Balmain Watch House is at 179 Darling Sreet, and was built in 1854 as a police lockup. Initially it was a single story building but with the population expansion it was extended to its present form in 1881. A new police station was opened further up Darling Street in 1887 but this Watch House remained a policeman's residence and overnight lockup until the 1920s. In the late 1920s it became solely a policeman's residence until 1965. It fell into disrepair after the last resident left and so it was that the Balmain Association with support from the National Trust appealed for its preservation and taking it over saved the building.

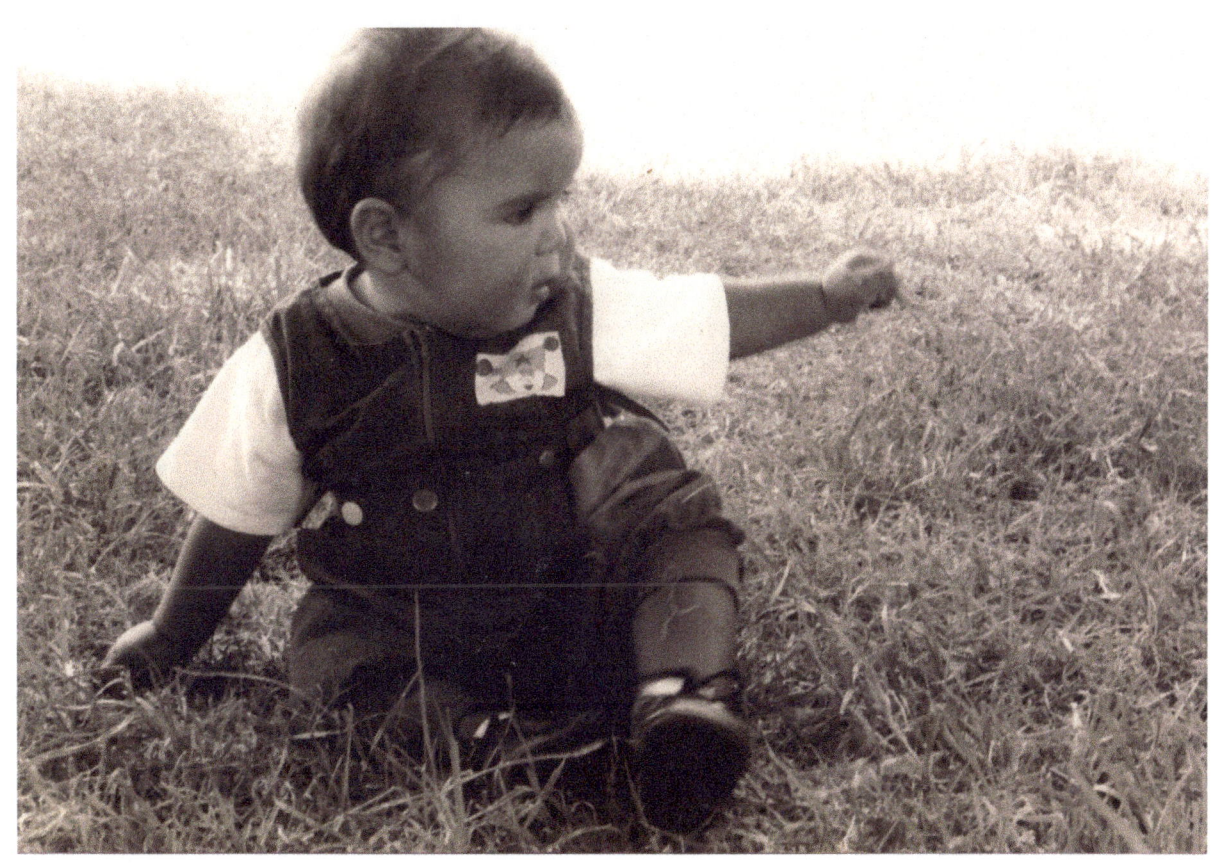

WOONUN ~ "WHISPERING OAK" (1992)
Photograph : Janet Scott

In April, 1992 Janet took a series of photos of 10 month old Woonun Edwin Willoughby in Snails Bay Park opposite "STUDIO FACADE". Woonun is the son of Narranga mother, award winning artist and author of BARDOO MAI & OTHER INDIGENOUS THINGS, Patrice Kunoth Power, adopted daughter of Anmatyerre actress and politician Dr. Rose Kunoth Monks OAM (1937 - 2022) who starred in the film JEDDA (1955). His father is Pitjantjantjara and Mirning dreaming, Hall of Fame musician and lyricist Bart Willoughby who was born at Koonibba Aboriginal Mission and was a first in many areas of Aboriginal music both nationally and internationally including winning the inaugural Aria Award in 1993 for Outstanding Contribution to Indigenous Music in Australia.

INVITATION to the Opening of their Mixed Exhbiition
on Tuesday, 14th December, 1993

CLEMENCY BROWNE   JANET SCOTT
KAY SINGLETON-KELLER   MICHAEL WRIGHT

THE BALMAIN WATCHHOUSE GALLERY
179 Darling Street, Balmain 2041

In 1993 Janet was seeking an appropriate person to paint for her entry to the 1994 Archibald Prize and I suggested Kevin's friend Justine Saunders. KK had first worked with Justine on a commercial in 1974 and formed a friendship and sporadic working relationship that lasted over 40 years throughout both of their immense bodies of work in the Australian media industries. Justine was the leading First Nation actress in both theatre and film for approximately 30 years. Her last production with Kevin was Brian Syron's feature film JINDALEE LADY (1992) on which Kevin J. Kearney was Executive Producer / Sound Designer and Justine Saunders OAM (1953 - 2007), a member of the Woppaburra from the Kanomie people of Great Keppel Island in Queensland, was Indigenous Affairs & Public Relations.

Janet extended the invitation to Justine to sit for her and her invitation was shyly accepted by Justine who said she had never had her portrait painted before.

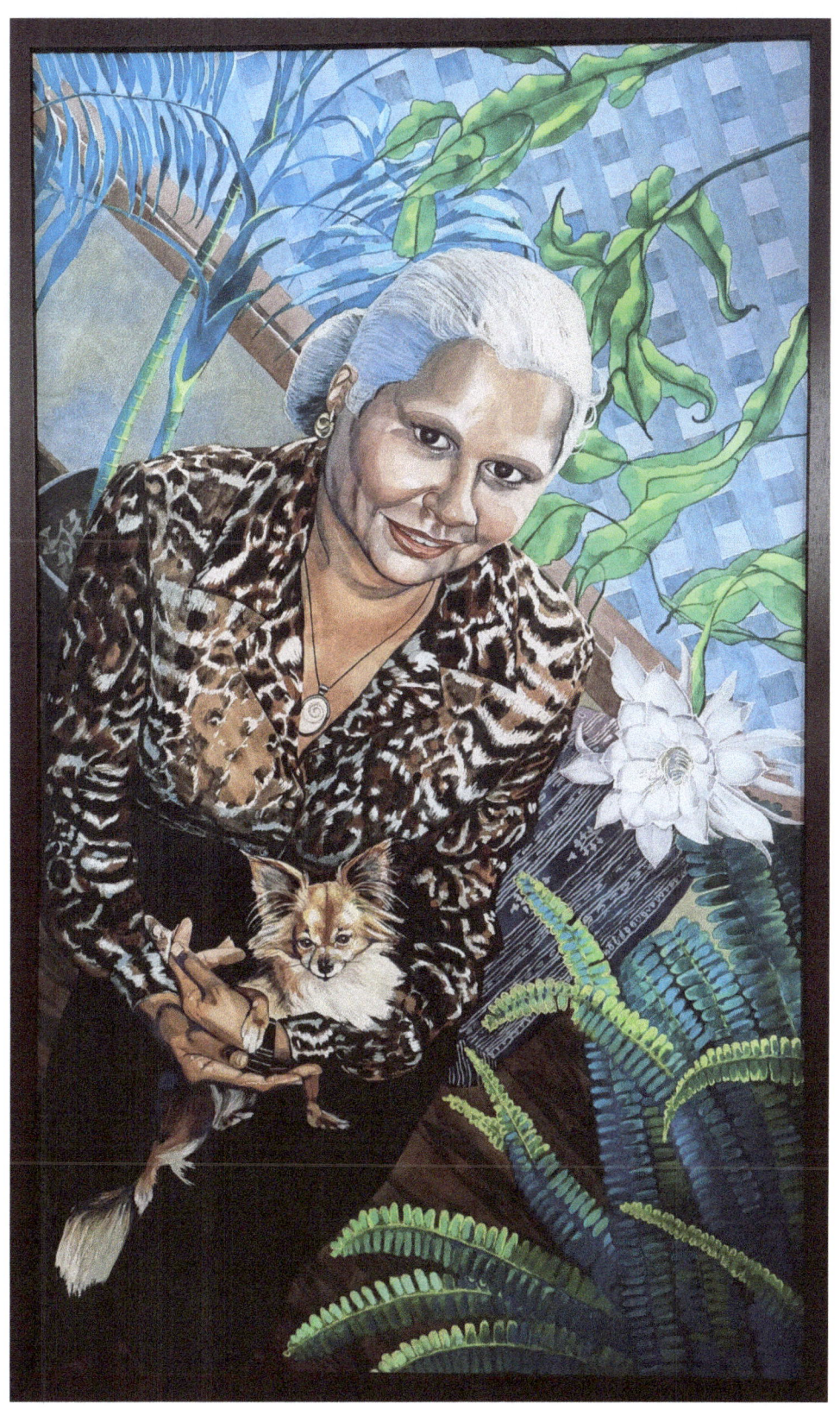

JUSTINE SAUNDERS, OAM (1994)
Artist : Janet Scott
Medium : Acrylic on paper - Size : 1065 x 1815 mm
Photograph by: Krissy Clark
artbykrissyclark@outlook.com

75

I believe Janet's portrait of Justine Saunders OAM has proved to be historic in two ways : Firstly, it is Justine's first and only portrait painted from real life. Even the National Portrait Gallery holds no paintings of this iconic First Nation actress and has only a location photo still (printed in 2003) dated 1994 from the television mini series HEARTLAND (1994) by the renowned photographer Juno Gemes.

Secondly, Janet's painting of Justine has formed part of the history of JINDALEE LADY the first feature film with First Nation "Above the Line" and crew who are all listed on IMDb

1. Director Birripi / Eora / Australian Brian Syron (1934 - 1993)
2. Music director and composer Pitjantjantjara / Mirning musician Bart Willoughby
3. Costumes designer Eora / Australian Stephen Fitzgerald (1955 - 1995)

4. Bangarra Dance Theatre in their first professioal appearance.
5. Clapper/Loader Bunjalung (now author) George Bostock
6. Best Boy Eora Brendan Reid (now cinematographer)
7. Grip Eora based Jason Webb
8. Woppaburra Indigenous Affairs & Public Relations & actress Justine Saunders (1953 - 2007)

Justine Saunders received
The inaugural 1985 Aboriginal Artist of the Year Award
1991 Medal of the Order of Australia
and
The 1999 Red Ochre Award.

In 1999 Kevin and I were invited to join an exuberant Justine, her mother Heather, Peter Whittle and other close friends when she received the Arts Council of Australia's Red Ochre Award but within a couple of years her health had begun to deteriorate and she retired with her partner actor / producer Peter Whittle to their home near Deerubin (aka the Hawkesbury River).

It was at Ocean Shores, perhaps around 2014, that Janet gave Justine's portrait to me and asked me to see if there were any organisations or family that might like to take the portrait. I have tried both options without success. So just recently I have had the portrait framed and at least I will enjoy looking at it until I find Jussie a home.

In 1994 Janet joined a group exhibition of prints, paintings and sculptures with, again, fellow artist Clemency Browne plus Ewa Wiodarczyk and Michael Wright which opened at the Balmain Watchhouse on Friday November 6th, 1994

Wednesday 15th January, 1986
Akea and Janet invite you to a "PRAWNS IN THE PARK"
to celebrate Akea's 4th birthday and MIDSUMMER
Please bring
a plate, a bottle, a deckchair& the family
We will bring the chocolate crackles
Cnr. Grove and Bay Sts, Birchgrove.

GALLERY REOPENS AFTER 10 YEARS …

"…Janet Scott   says Studio Facade is back in business because interest in the arts is growing ..THE SECRET LANGUAGE OF TREES will be the first exhibition for the reopening and Janet will exhibit her own work at Studio Facade for the first time…the works are centred around the theme of trees and nature …"I began a series of paintings in which I slowly began the process of lettng go of realism and painting the skin of the trees."……

Exract of article by Gabrielle Lawrence

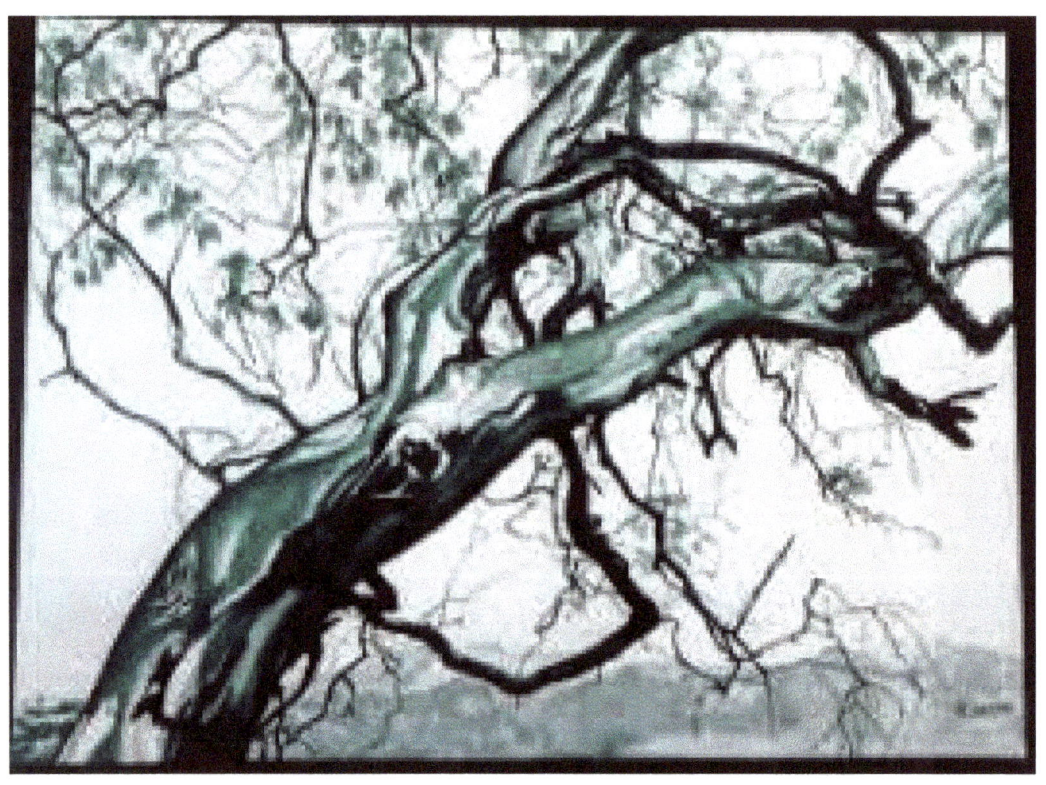

Artist : Janet Scott

STUDIO FACADE
Artist : Janet Scott
invites you to an exhibition of
recent unframed works on paper
by Janet Scott
THE SECRET LANGUAGE OF TREES
Thursday, 27 March, 1997

OBJECTS OF DESIRE (2000)

Artist	Janet Scott
Gallery	Gallery East
	21 Burnie Street, Clovelly
Manager	John Butterworth
Date	19th October, 1995 - 29th October, 2000

"Magic realism as a sensual delight ...
This exhibition of small works is art as Objects of Desire. The works are delightfully textural...intimate in capture and in context, creating a sensual glow that will put a smile on your face. The textural skin tones have been created over many months by building up layers of oil glazes over a base of egg tempera . The result magic realism as sensual delight."

"Technically excellent" - Geoffrey De Groen
"In terms of technique she is highly professional" - Ron Saw - SMH
"...magic realism with a heightened sense of the ordinary ...her work as a whole is a celebration; a refined affinity with the examined, in thoughtful collaboration with the imagined." - Heather Ellyard, ABC
"Admirable works these!" Nancy Borlase, SMH

Around 1996 1997 Janet decided to leave Sydney and move north. She was going to buy a Kombi van and, from her proposed new base, travel around Australia on painting trips. Her first move was to plan her mission. Janet's family were now adults and so her move north was going to be a solo one - in fact her first time living alone in at least 30 years. There was quite a lot of organising to do including the selling of her property in Birch and all things excess to her next location.

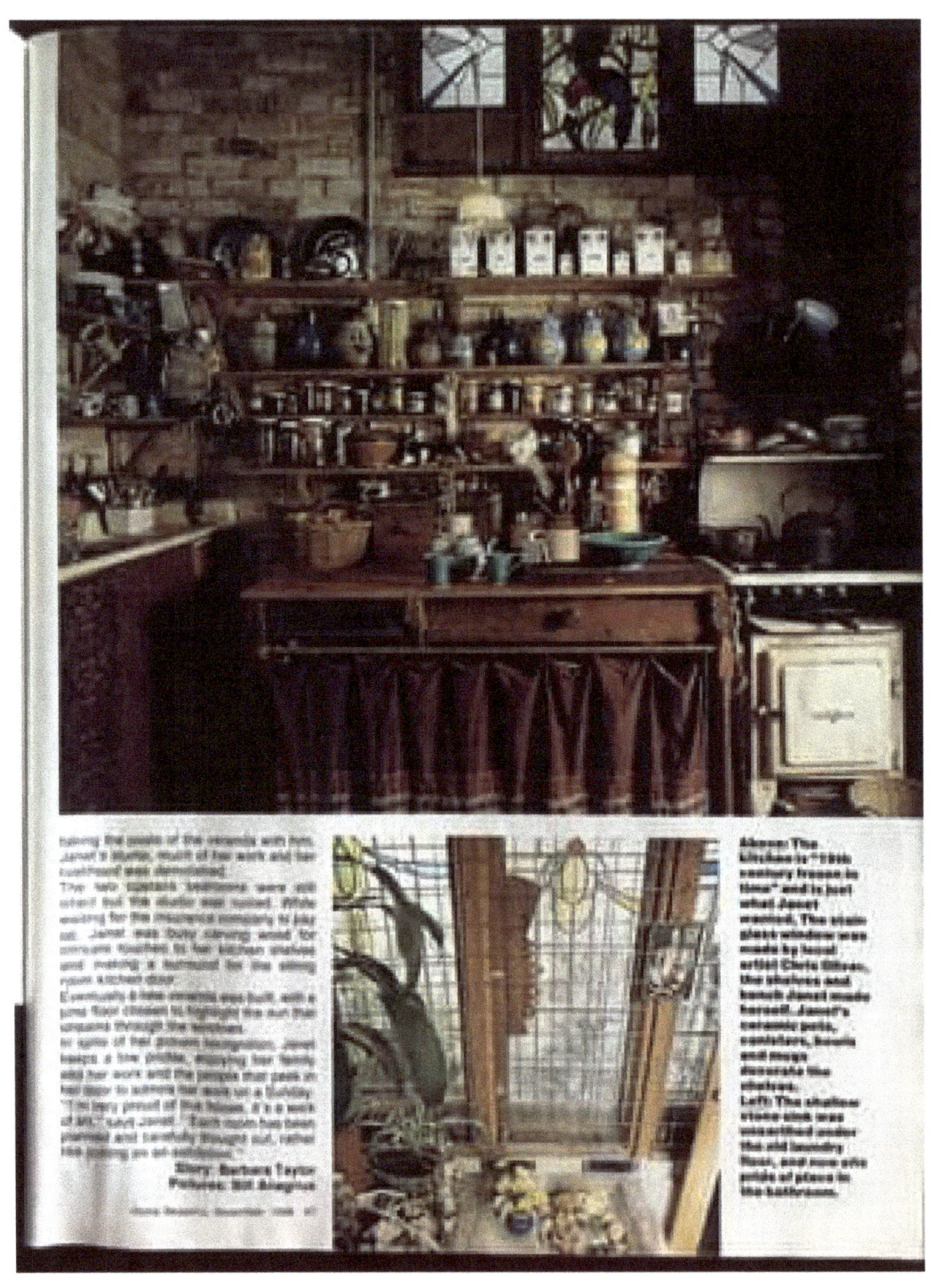

Janet Scott's kitchen
HOME BEAUTIFUL - Nov. 1988

Although it is hard to see - but the middle window above the kitchen shelves is : 17. Jane le Rossignol's - "Rosella" from the LEAP INTO SPRING WITH A LAUGH EXHIBITION at STUDIO FACADE which opened on 26 September, 1982 . Janet took this beautiful piece with her when she moved North.

The family made the following comments on Jessica's Facebook page regarding this wonderful photograph of Janet's interior decor which apeared in a magazine ...

Jessica Douglas
This is the kitchen I learnt to cook in. My Mum wanted to recreate her granny's kitchen. I wanted the mod cons with my reno, mind you 1970s brick has a different patina from 1880's sandstone! I've also had no strong desire to have a gas cooker after singeing my arm hairs and eyebrows cooking on the Kooka. But I look at it now and it's so my mum. Totally individual and rather beautiful.

Miranda Jane
Awww I reckon that's why I could cook so well with my terrible stove! Thanks mum - so much cheese on toast consumed - it was great when she returned from Bali with the hibachi and satay on the mind ... well done mum xx
PS best gado gado and peanut sauce ever!

Akea Scott
Still love that kitchen💜

Susan Scott
As you say Jess - it was so your mum!

Alex Scott
I loved cooking in your mums kitchen as a kid.

April, 2022

Once the house was sold Janet sent invitations to friends and invited interested people to :-
AN AUCTION
of
THE ART AND EFFECTS OF JANET SCOTT
on 30 March, 2000
@ "Studio Facade"
37 Grove St., BIRCHGROVE

So along with many of Janet's large group of friends and other "interested people" I attended the auction and bought my piece of Janet's collection …

No. 6.   Main Bedroom
Item No. 145
"Brianne with Bangles"
Pencil on Paper .. 31.5 x 30.5
Price $40.00 - framed
Ref. "THE PAST IN PASSING" (2019) ISBN 978 0 359 99001 6 : p.221

Janet also asked Kevin if he would film the event which he did,   filming historic short interviews with buyers like Roger Foley (aka Ellis D Fogg), Adrian Rawlins and Martin Sharp.

THE SALE OF JANET SCOTT'S COLLECTION - (2000)
Auctioneer   Janet Scott
Producer   Janet Scott
Director / Camera   Kevin Kearney
Shoot date   30.3.2000

Tape of this production is held by Janet Scott

Sometime following this activity Janet moved to Katya Court, Ocean Shores, Byron Shire north across the Brunswick River.

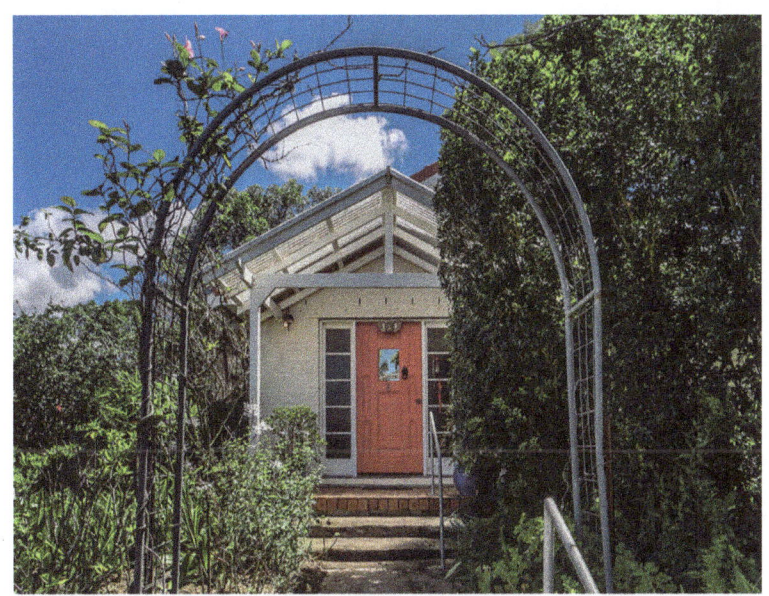

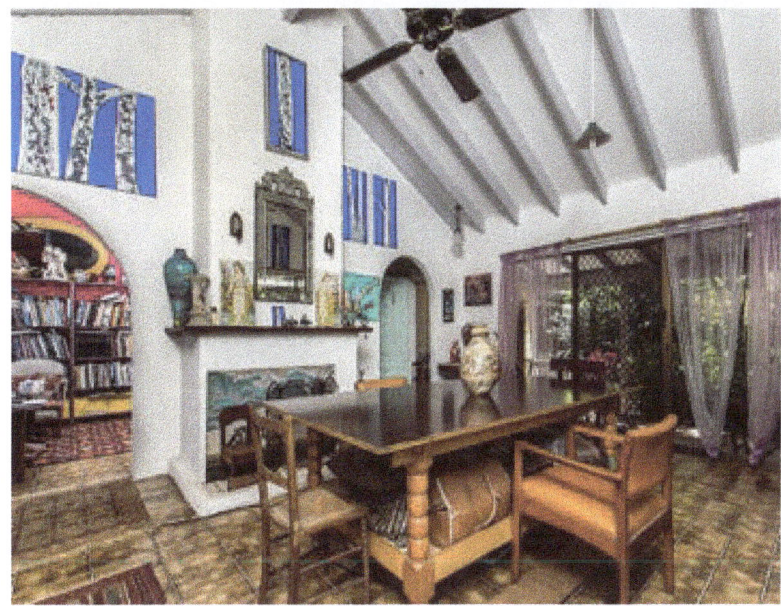

Photographer unknown

She did buy her Kombi van which she upgraded for her new adventure, thrilled to make the move and excitedly talking of her plans to travel around Australia. Although Janet's visit to the Northern Territory to proffer her apology to the Aboriginal people was a journey that consequently gave Janet a beautiful series of Outback paintings her extended travels throughout Australia were not to be.

As usual Janet added another craft to the wood carving of her picture frames by joining a woodworking group in Mullumbimby and turning her prodigious talent to making some beautiful pieces of furniture for her home. Her new house was on a hill looking out to the ocean and Janet designed her garden with a huge herb plot, a pond and the trees that she loved.

In 2000 I moved from Rozelle to Humpybong Esplanade, Redcliffe which is north of Brisbane and on the old highway was probably about 3 hours each way from Ocean Shores so I did not see Janet as frequently as I did when I just lived up the road in Gipps Street, Birchgrove. She continued to do her painting and I still loved to visit and see what it was that Janet was working on. It was always an amazingly creative experience - in fact I thought that she did some of her best work in her new house yet all this work with brushes and hammers etc. was having a deleterious effect on her hands.

We kept in touch by email but unfortunately as time went on Janet became increasingly frail and she was finding her house in Ocean Shores a little too large to handle alone. Of course, she did get help but with all largish houses they really need much more input to keep them on an even keel.

Then presciently in 2015, two days before I was due to fly to Waialae Iki, Oahu for business in the States I felt an urgent pull to visit Janet. I arrived in the midst of her sale of furniture and other items that were surplus to her needs. She told me she had tried to get in touch and was moving to Waratah Avenue, Woy Woy to be nearer her grandchildren and beloved daughters Jessica, Miranda and Akea. She had bought a much smaller home with little or no garden and would have help in the house with a live-in couple but I could see that Janet was now very, very frail.

This proved to be the last time that I saw Janet in person.   Kevin's health was also waning and for the next few years I was caught up with hospitals and doctors for Kevin and so I was unable to visit Janet in Woy Woy. Both Janet Scott (my friend of 45 years) and Kevin Joseph Kearney (my partner of 55 years) died within months of each other ...

Janet Catherine Scott
(Janey).
20.8.1941 – 23.4.2018

Late of Woy Woy. Formerly of Ocean Shores, 'Studio Facade' Birchgrove, Aranda, Belconnen, Canberra and 'Carwoola' Bungendore.
Dearly loved mother, sister, grandmother, aunt, activist, artist, friend and free spirit.

The following are some of the artistic activities of
JANET SCOTT

1. Painting
2. Drawing
3. Pottery
4. Posters
5. Illustrations
6. Books - writing + illustrations
7. DVDs - e.g.. iNYOMAN GUNARSA - ARTIST
8. "Studio Facade" - Janet Scott's gallery
9. Furniture
10. Wood carving
11. Exhibitions
12. Canberra - Festivals
13. Masks
14. Galleries

>   Aces Art Shop - Ace Bourke
>   Hogarth Gallery - Clive Evatt
>   Robin Gibson Gallery - Robin Gibson
>   Bellair Gallery, Toronto, Canada
>   Studio Facade
>   Antares Gallery
>   Balmain Watchhouse
>   Gallery East

15. Photography
16. Canberra - Stage Productions

. . . .

I am sure there are more areas of Janet Scott's amazingly eclectic career that I am unaware of and I agree with Jessica Douglas, her eldest daughter, that a paper should be included in any book that relates to the period in which Janet worked, outlining the difficulties that she and other women experienced in their early careers as female artists. This was a period when it was not considered at all the thing for women to be ... but attitudes began changing in the 1970s...e.g. Robin Gibson, Clive Evatt and Ace Bourke are a few men who exhibited both Janet's work and that of other women artists.

The following are a number of current Australian exhibitions devoted to women and short extracts from papers by women who have studied the presence (or lack thereof) of women artists ...

1. KNOW MY NAME - AUSTRALIAN WOMEN ARTISTS AT THE NATIONAL GALLERY OF AUSTRALIA (2020 - 2021) - Canberra
2. FEM-aFFINITY (2021) Riddoch Arts & Cultural Centre, Victoria
3. BECOMING MODERN - AUSTRALIAN WOMEN ARTISTS 1920 - 1950 (2019) - Ballarat Art Gallery
4. CONTEMPORARY AUSTRALIA : WOMEN - Queensland Art Gallery
5. AUSTRALIAN WOMEN ARTISTS, ONE HUNDRED YEARS : 1840 - 1940 - Travelling Exhibition
6. HILMA af KLINT - Art Gallery of New South Wales (June-Sept. 2021)
and
7. WOMEN IN AUSTRALIAN ART
   National Association for the Visual Arts (NAVA)

10 WOMEN ARTISTS WITH MAJOR SHOWS IN 2021
NAVA CONTEMPORARY

"In 1985 the collective of feminists artists GUERRILLA GIRLS asked 'How many women had one person exhibitions at NYC museums last year?'   The answer was just one at MoMA and zero at the Guggenheim, the Met and the Whitney.

Over three decades later the art world contiues to be undoubtedly ruled by men. Only 11 percent of all museum acquisitions between 2009 and 2019 were pieces by women, and female artists' works are still valued less than those of their male peers. Never mind the disparities when it comes to women of color.

And yet, putting this list together to commemorate Women's History Month provided a small sense of confidence that things are slowly but surely changing for the better. From Sydney to San Francisco, a wide array of women artists from diverse backgrounds are increasingly being recognized for their talents with numerous major female - focused retrospectives and solo show at museums

Salome Goez-Upegui - March 8, 2021

PROFESSOR GRISELDA POLLOCK
Professor Pollock's credits confirmed, among other roles, she was the Founding director of the Centre for Cultural Analysis, Theory and History at the University of Leeds with an interest and involvement in the women's movement, the world of art history and its percenption of women. Professor Pollock wrote :

"I first became aware of the absence of women in art history while studying at university in the late 60s.
"I wasn't being taught about women artists, or they were mentioning them only to belittle them," she recalls.

Pollock told Namila Benson on The Art Show.

"I decided to go to the National Gallery [London] and look for women artists, and there they were [but] in the basement, not on show ... there were only nine of them in the whole of the National Gallery,"

This discovery sent Pollock on a journey into other basements and archives, to find women and write them back into history.

This year, her decades of work in this area was recognised when she became the first art historian to win the Holberg Prize, a 6 million Norwegian krone ($900,000) annual award for a scholar in the arts and humanities, social sciences, law or theology.

Despite the win, Pollock is humble, calling herself an "an impassioned art historian, working to save the women artists that I see around me from being delivered to the dustbin of history in their lifetimes — which is still happening..."

MEANJIN

2019 research by art agency IN OTHER WORDS and ARTNET NEWS found that women artists represent just 2 per cent of the global art market, despite dominating tertiary art programs.

However, the range of choice available (to women) was often circumscribed by the little attention hitherto given many of these women.

This means that while a proportion of the more prominent painters — such as Grace Cossington Smith, Margaret Preston, Thea Proctor and Grace Crowley — are represented by a substantial body of work, enabling us to trace certain preoccupations and developments in their art, other careers, such as those of Jane Price, Clara Southern, Jane Sutherland, Mildred Lovett and Nancy Guest, are virtually closed to us. Not only do we lack a sizeable number of works by these artists from which we could assess the standard or scope of their art, but the paucity of biographical documentation makes their lives and personalities even more fugitive.

It is this kind of lacuna which makes the attempt to assess both collectively, and historically the contribution made by the women artists of this country to Australian art history so imperative. That is the crux of the exhibition. It was its initial impetus, and remains the continuing dynamic.

Janine Burke - Summer 1975

WOMEN IN AUSTRALIAN ART

Women in the art world first began to protest against the inequities of representation and opportunity as part of 'second wave feminism' in the 1960s, when artists like Vivienne Binns and Juno Gemes were giving performances and staging exhibitions about feminist issues. This was taking place during a period when broader civil rights activism was raising issues of Aboriginal land rights and gay and lesbian discrimination and protests were being staged against the Vietnam War.

In particular, around the time of the International Women's Year in 1975, new structures and mechanisms were being used to create change. The Women's Art Movement, set up in 1974 with groups formed in Sydney, Canberra, Melbourne, and Adelaide, began with the aim of promoting women artists, exposing problems of discrimination and providing a sense of solidarity and mutual support, which resulted in a surge of creative action and artwork.

In 1975, the Australian Women's Art Register was established by artists in Melbourne, to record and promote the work of Australian-based women artists. The Register continues today, now holding a collection of images dating back to 1840, which document the cultural contribution of Australian women artists and their art practices. It has just celebrated its 40th anniversary with a multi-venue curated festival of feminist visual art events across Melbourne.

Tamara Winikoff
March 23, 2016
National Association for the Visual Arts (NAVA)

SHORT CV - JANET SCOTT (August 1941 - April 2018)

AWARDS
1965   Australian National University Art Prize
        Janet Scott's work is represented in the Australian National
        University collection

SOLO EXHIBITION
1967   Silk Screened Fabrics - Cinema Centre Gallery,
            Canberra
1970   Paintings - Australian Sculpture Gallery, Canberra
1975   "Quadrant' - Drawings - Hogarth Gallery, Sydney
1979   Robin Gibson Gallery, Sydney
1982   Bellair Gallery, Toronto, Canada
1983   Antares Gallery, Sydney
1985   Studio Facade, Cnr. Bay & Grove, Sts, Birchgrove
1997   The Secret Life of Trees
2000   Objects of Desire

GROUP EXHIBITIONS
1981   Bellair Gallery, Toronto, Canada
1981   Toronto International Art Fair
1982   "Leap Into Spring with a Laugh", Studio Facade, Sydney
1983   Antares Gallery
1990   Pots 'n' Prints for Christmas, The Balmain Watchhouse,
            Balmain
1994   The Balmain Watchhouse, Balmain

SPECIAL EVENTS
1973   "EXPLORATIONS" with Youth Theatre for Kids,
            Canberra

1973	Youth Theatre and Salt Workshop Association . from Sydney, Melbourne and Canberra combined senses ranging from delight to disgust - televised by Australian Broadcasting Commission - sponsored by Australia Council for the Arts
1974	Salt Production of "Jam, Jelly and Bread", a 3 D show sponsored by Australia Council for the Arts
1976	Moved to Sydney
1976-78	Studied Photography at the Australian Centre for Photography Studied dance with Lindsay Kemp
1980	Founded Studio Facade, Sydney "a small gallery in search of a sense of humour"
1982	Co-founder Antares Gallery, Sydney "an artists' co-operative"
1984	Nyoman Gunarsa - An Artist (1984) - documentary
1984	Nyoman Gunarsa @ Studio Facade

TEACHING

1969 - 1971	Teaching painting, drawing & printmaking @ Canberra Technical College
1972 - 1975	Canberra Art Club
1976 - 1977	Willoughby Arts Workshop, North Sydney

OTHER

1990	April Issue - "Open Road" - "Janet Scott's Pots"
1984	STUDIO FACADE was co-producer on a 30 minute documentary NYOMAN GUNARSA - ARTIST (1979)
1990	THE CHRONICLES OF ICARUS Retold, illustrated and published by Janet Scott Designed by Jennifer Gormley ISBN 0 646 00831 5

SOME BOOKS

FRAGMENTS OF ACID & REMNANTS OF LOVE -
First edition - Private publication - Limited edition 1 of 1 (1983)
Third edition - ISBN 978-1-4477-9260-4 (2021) p.32

SUNDAY WITH AKIA - For Akea Scott (1985) -Limited Edition - 1 of 1

KEVIN KEARNEY, SOUND DESIGNER, AUDIO ARTIST & ANALOGUE LOCATION
SOUND RECORDIST
Vol. 2 Part 2 - First Edition ISBN - 978-1-387-74488-6 (2016)
pp. 46 / 77 /109 / 129 / 135 / 138 / 268

KEVIN KEARNEY, SOUND DESIGNER, AUDIO ARTIST & ANALOGUE LOCATION
SOUND RECORDIST
Vol. 2 Part 1 - Second Edition - ISBN 978-1-387-65469 - 7 (2018)
pp. 144 / 200 / 269 -270 / 376

THE PAST IN PASSING (2019)
ISBN : 978-0-359-99001-6 pp. 93, 141, 144, 146, 193, 205, 217, 218, 221

RUNNING THE MONSOON - Medan to Jakarta Indonesia 1971 (2020)
ISBN: 978 1 008 98451 - 6 pp. 8, 67

briann - Some Restored Photographs - 1959 - 1970 (2021)
ISBN : 978-1-326007848-5 pp.150 - 154

JT + KK = 2 MATES -
JACK THOMPSON, AO & KEVIN KEARNEY
Part One (2020)
ISBN 978-1-008-98090-7 pp.96 / 102 / 174

JT + KK = 2 MATES -
JACK THOMPSON, AO & KEVIN KEARNEY
Part Two (2020)
ISBN 978-1-326-25051-5 : pp 164 /168 / 170 / 197 / 218 / 223 / 230 / 247 / 251 / 280-281 /
302 / 303 / 334

JT + KK = 2 MATES -
JACK THOMPSON, AO & KEVIN KEARNEY
Part Three (2022)
2nd Edition (2021) ISBN ; 978-1-4709-1001-3 : pp 49 / 54 / 61 /78 / 82/111 - 112 / 133 / 164

THE COMPLETE ARCHIVE
OF THE
ARTISTIC OEUVRE
OF
JANET CATHERINE SCOTT
aka
JANET C. SCOTT
JANET SCOTT
J.C. SCOTT
&
JANEY DOUGLAS

IS HELD IN A PRIVATE COLLECTION
and

© to Janet's work is held by
her daughters
Jessica Douglas, Miranda Douglas & Akea Scott